pg - 29 - ६१

D0085537

ABUSE IN THE WORKPLACE

ABUSE IN THE WORKPLACE

Management Remedies and Bottom Line Impact

EMILY S. BASSMAN

QUORUM BOOKS

Westport, Connecticut • London

HF
5548.85
.B365
1992

Fairleigh Dickinson University
Library

Rutherford, N.J.

Library of Congress Cataloging-in-Publication Data

Bassman, Emily S.
  Abuse in the workplace : management remedies and bottom line
impact / Emily S. Bassman.
    p.   cm.
  Includes bibliographical references and index.
  ISBN 0–89930–673–X (alk. paper)
  1. Job stress. 2. Job satisfaction. 3. Organizational change.
I. Title.
  HF5548.85.B365   1992
  658.3—dc20   92–7505

British Library Cataloguing in Publication Data is available.

Copyright © 1992 by Emily S. Bassman

All rights reserved. No portion of this book may be
reproduced, by any process or technique, without the
express written consent of the publisher.

Library of Congress Catalog Card Number: 92–7505
ISBN: 0–89930–673–X

First published in 1992

Quorum Books, 88 Post Road West, Westport, CT 06881
An imprint of Greenwood Publishing Group, Inc.

Printed in the United States of America

♾™

The paper used in this book complies with the
Permanent Paper Standard issued by the National
Information Standards Organization (Z39.48–1984).

10 9 8 7 6 5 4 3 2 1

To Shirley E. Bassman

Contents

Acknowledgments   ix

Introduction: What is Employee Abuse?   xi

Part I. Individual Acts of Abuse   1

1. What Does Employee Abuse Look Like?   3

2. Traditional Forms of Abuse   27

3. The Dynamics of Employee Abuse   43

4. Social and Behavioral Aspects of Abusive Relationships   51

Part II. Institutional Abuse   65

5. The Ethics of Employee Treatment   67

6. Overwork and the Workaholic Organization   77

7. Policies, Procedures, and Management Practices   93

8. Potential for New Forms of Abuse: Employee Testing   107

9. Potential for New Forms of Abuse: Employee Privacy   123

Part III. Impact on Organizations 135

10. The Costs of Employee Abuse 137

11. Corporate Response to Employee Abuse 153

Part IV. Solutions 163

12. Guidance for Employers 165

13. A Model for Examining the Corporate Culture 181

14. The Road Ahead 193

Selected Bibliography 197

Index 199

Acknowledgments

This book has been in the making for a number of years. It has been a very special project for me, because it was an opportunity to integrate my experience in the business world, my knowledge as a psychologist, and my values as a human being. Many people have contributed to the formation of the ideas expressed in these pages, whether or not they knew it at the time. To my colleagues, mentors, friends, and family members who enriched my intellectual and ethical understanding of the issues, I owe a debt of special thanks. I certainly hope that I contributed to their development in equally satisfying ways.

Throughout this book, I relate anecdotes and stories of mistreatment and misunderstandings in the workplace. All of the incidents recounted are true, to the best of my knowledge. In some cases, the stories came from publications, and in these cases the references are cited. Where there are no references, the story was related to me. These have been edited only to remove any identifying information. I would like to thank everyone who shared their stories with me. I can't name them, but they know who they are.

A special note of thanks goes to Manny London for his intellectual and moral support, as well as for soliciting from his students at the Business School at the State University of New York a number of stories about abuse in the workplace. Manny was also one of the best bosses I have ever had. I feel privileged to have had the opportunity to learn from him.

Thanks to my editor, Eric Valentine, for his enthusiasm about the idea of doing this book, and his patience and encouragement during the process of bringing it into being.

Introduction: What is Employee Abuse?

It has always been the case that some bosses are abusive to their employees. Indeed, in American culture Mr. Dithers, Dagwood Bumstead's boss in the popular comic strip "Blondie," could be said to be the archetype of the abusive boss. However, the events of the last decade have increased the frequency and severity of such abuse in the workplace, as well as its subtlety and sophistication, especially in corporations. This book is intended to alert employers, especially upper-level management in corporations, of the potential for this abuse and the conditions that support it. This book also will serve to provide guidance in creating an environment in which abuse does not occur, or in coping with the problems created by abuse if it has already surfaced.

What constitutes employee abuse? In this book, it is any behavior on the part of a supervising manager that is aimed at controlling an employee and that results in, or is intended to result in, the employee's loss of self-esteem, self-confidence, feeling of competence, or control over his or her work or personal life, and the employee's increased dependence on the manager. Employee abuse, in this context, does not necessarily involve discrimination on the basis of age, gender, race, or any other kind of diversity, although it may. There also need not be any physical abuse involved, although that may be present in some cases. The abuse discussed in this book is more mental and emotional in nature, and always involves the use and misuse of the power that the manager has over the subordinate. Due to renewed pressures on companies today to improve performance, new stresses are introduced into the relationship between manager and employee. Since the manager holds the power in the relationship, the employee is most often the victim when these stresses cause the relationship to become dysfunctional. In other words, employee abuse creates a hostile work environment.

The damaging effects of a hostile work environment have been recognized legally in the context of sexual harassment. The legal definition of sexual harassment has evolved over recent years. The most current definition is one that includes not only blatant threats of "Sleep with me or lose your job," but also situations in which a hostile work environment is maintained and contributes to making the victim uncomfortable at work. This book deals with a generic form of harassment, of which sexual harassment is only one variety. The National Organization for Women defines the environmental type of sexual harassment as a "sexually intimidating, offensive work environment." Remove the word sexually from the definition, and you have a description of the work environment created by generic employee abuse. Some of the most identifiable kinds of employee abuse, such as discrimination and sexual harassment, are already illegal, although they continue to cause problems in the workplace. It is the less identifiable forms of abuse, those that result from a more generic type of abuse of power over other individuals, that round out the concept of generic employee abuse. Employees victimized by such abuse suffer just as intensely from the hostile environment in which they work as do victims of sexual harassment, but their situation has not yet been named or recognized by employers or the legal profession. This book attempts to recognize and name the phenomenon, as well as to expand the notion of a hostile work environment to include these more generic forms of employee abuse and harassment.

In contrast to sexual harassment, the content of other forms of generic employee abuse is likely to be much more directly work related, even performance related, resulting in a much more ambiguous situation for an employee. The supervisor has an acknowledged right, even an obligation, to evaluate a subordinate's performance. If sexual harassment can be so subtle as to cause employees to doubt their own perceptions and judgment, imagine the extent to which criticisms over performance could affect employees' confidence in their own judgment. A manager who uses power over a subordinate very likely will use performance assessments in attempts to control the employee, and these attempts are very likely to be successful. Unless the employee belongs to a protected class, it would be very difficult to attribute unfair treatment to anything specific. Even if the employee does belong to a protected class, it may be the case that the manager treats all subordinates equally badly, and so discrimination does not enter into the subordinate's assessment of what is going on.

In such a situation, the employee has no recourse. Usually, companies have no specific procedures to deal with generic employee abuse. If the employee complains about treatment from a manager, especially if that manager has judged the employee's performance to be poor, the employee has very little credibility and minimal power to influence managers at higher levels. The employee runs the risk that nothing will be done about the situation, while being branded as a troublemaker and a malcontent. Furthermore, the employee's relationship with his or her manager is likely to deteriorate still further after the employee's complaint, because the manager probably will be angry with the employee.

Another class of abuse is more institutional. Included here are aspects of the corporate culture as well as policies, procedures, and management practices that provide an environment supporting abuse. For instance, the workaholic culture found in so many American companies creates many opportunities for the abuse of employees. As another example, consider new benefits policies that use managed medical care. Employee choice of a physician frequently is denied, and serious questions have been raised about the quality of available care. Many of these plans make deductions from the fees paid to doctors when hospitalization is required. Although such plans are adopted to save medical costs and eliminate unnecessary medical procedures, their compensation system may also reward minimal care in some cases that could turn out to be quite serious and need aggressive care quickly.

These are important issues for employers to address, because they can have major bottom-line consequences. Some of the most direct costs associated with employee abuse can be seen in stress and disability claims, workers' compensation claims, medical costs, and lawsuits, including wrongful discharge. Other, more indirect costs are poor quality, high turnover, absenteeism, poor customer relationships, or even sabotage. Still more indirect costs lie in the "opportunity costs" of lowered employee commitment: lack of discretionary effort, commitments outside the job, time spent talking about the problem rather than working, and loss of creativity.

Just as other types of formerly taboo abusive relationships have come to light in recent years, the phenomenon of employee abuse is likely to surface as a major issue due to the growth of conditions that support it, and to the demographic and psychological characteristics of the present-day workforce. For instance, the support of one's immediate supervisor is essential to achieving a promotion (or merely to keeping one's job). This has effectively deterred employees from taking action concerning an abusive manager. However, the phenomenon of swelling numbers of baby boomers hitting midcareer in an era of corporate downsizing has resulted in widespread career plateauing. As increasing numbers of employees realize that their careers have plateaued, and that they won't be getting promoted anyway, the degree of control that managers can exercise by manipulating expectations will diminish.

This book will discuss employee abuse and the causes for its increase over the past decade, organizational factors that both promote it and prevent it from coming to light, and interventions necessary to prevent its occurrence or minimize the damage. Special attention will be given to organizational development issues such as quality, employee involvement, and managing diversity, for their influence in creating an environment that minimizes abusive practices.

The nature of this subject matter is volatile, even explosive. The nation recently witnessed just how explosive a sexual harassment charge can be during the Supreme Court confirmation hearings for Judge Clarence Thomas. Such charges often can bring up strong opinions regarding character, values, prejudices, guilt, fears, and so forth. It may be more comfortable to ignore these issues. Examining the circumstances surrounding a charge of abuse or harassment, even when one is not directly involved in those circumstances, forces one to hold up a mirror to one's own self and behavior. Reading about instances of abusive behavior in this book will raise some of the same issues for the reader. This book is not an exposé. It is meant to be a professional treatment of a very complex, difficult, ambiguous, and important problem in workplaces today. It does not assume that the abuse of employees is intentional and malicious behavior. It may be in some cases, but in many others it is not. The important point is that abuse need not be intentional to be damaging—to the employee and to the employer. This book begins on this premise.

Part I
Individual Acts of Abuse

This section concentrates on abusive behavior from a variety of perspectives. Chapter 1 describes abusive treatment of subordinates, focusing on the characteristics of employee abuse. Employee abuse is categorized into a number of distinct and identifiable kinds of behavior. Descriptions of each kind are given, based on real incidents from many sources. Examples are taken from manufacturing companies, service companies, small businesses, educational institutions, health service organizations, and public service agencies.

Chapter 2 focuses on discrimination and sexual harassment, the more traditional types of abuse seen in organizations. Chapter 3 compares abusive relationships in the workplace to other kinds of abusive relationships. Similarities in the behavior of both the victim and the perpetrator, and the secrecy that surrounds the relationship are described. The nature of power in organizations also contributes to the atmosphere of secrecy, effectively preventing employees from taking action against their abusers.

Chapter 4 explores, from a perspective of social psychology and social learning, the persistent use of punishment to control behavior. Also reviewed is the unexpected finding that only a few external demands are needed to elicit extremes of abusive behavior from normal people. Implications for the workplace are discussed.

1

What Does Employee Abuse Look Like?

During the early 1990s, a growing awareness of the extent and impact of employee abuse surfaced. Before this time, publications addressing mistreatment of employees dealt with specific and previously identified forms of abuse: discrimination on the basis of age, race, or gender, and sexual harassment. Numerous articles and books were published on stress in the workplace, stress-related disability and workers' compensation claims, and the effects of management style on productivity and job satisfaction, but they described each of these phenomena in isolation, rather than as part of a newly identified behavioral pattern.

One notable exception is a special report by Lombardo and McCall (1984), which examines the situation of working for an intolerable boss. This study was part of a larger, long-term study, conducted by the Center for Creative Leadership, of successful executives in large organizations. Executives were interviewed about their experiences working for an intolerable boss. Several types of intolerable bosses were identified, as well as strategies used by the executives to cope with them. If they were lucky, they learned something—how *not* to behave as a boss. However, the authors point out that, since only successful executives were interviewed about this experience, there is no way to know how destructive some of these bosses were. They may have destroyed innumerable careers, even though some subordinates managed to survive and succeed.

One of the next publications to deal directly with employee abuse is a special report in the BNA Special Report Series on Work and Family entitled "Violence and Stress: The Work/Family Connection" (1990). This document describes how managers abuse their employees, attributing the cause of the behavior to the managers' own histories of being abused as children. It also discusses how negative characteristics dominate when a manager is under pressure. Strandell (1991) published a short article on ethics in a management journal in which she identifies the problem of managers victimizing their employees on a daily basis. Another contribution to this area is an article by Wilson (1991) describing workplace trauma resulting from employers' continual and deliberate malicious treatment of employees.

Such management abuse of employees is not new. As previously noted, this behavior has always existed. What is new in many companies today is an environment of unending and relentless pressure, due to increased competition and ineffective strategies for increasing competitiveness. Under such conditions, many more managers have reverted to negative management techniques and abusive tactics.

CHARACTERISTICS OF EMPLOYEE ABUSE

Intent versus Impact

What kind of supervisor behavior is abusive? Many managers reading this will be tempted to stop here, because they can honestly say that they have no intention of abusing their subordinates. Unfortunately, this does not guarantee that their behavior will not be abusive. What makes behavior abusive is its effect on subordinates. If subordinates feel abused, the supervisor's behavior likely is abusive, regardless of intentions. This thought was expressed effectively by one manager, who said, "I know a lot of people think I'm a son-of-a-bitch to work for, but I don't mean to be!"

It is necessary to make a distinction between the *intent* and the *impact* of behavior. This distinction can be made with regard to any human behavior. What message did the person intend to send by a given action? What message actually came across to others? Since people cannot perceive what another person is thinking (at least, most people can't), attributions and inferences must be made from the other person's behavior. Sometimes those inferences are accurate, sometimes they are not, and we often become confused about this state of affairs. We assume that we know what the other person means; it seems obvious. We judge the intent of others by the impact of their behavior on us. We also assume that others know why we behave in certain ways, forgetting that they do not have access to our thoughts, as we do. Since we understand why we are doing a certain action, or what message we intend to send, we assume that others know this too. Therefore, we cannot fully appreciate the unintended impact that our behavior may have on others.

Confusion between intent and impact often leads subordinates to infer malevolent motivation on the part of bosses, and leads bosses to wonder why subordinates do not understand why they do what they do. Frequently the two parties, if they discuss the situation, communicate on two different levels of meaning. The subordinate talks about what the boss did, his or her interpretation of the action, and the impact it had on him or her. The boss explains why he or she took the action, assuming that others already know the reason. The subordinate is oblivious to the boss's motivation, and the boss is oblivious to the impact of his or her behavior on others.

Bosses must recognize that it usually does not matter why they did what they did, if the negative impact is great enough. Explanations of behavior that subordinates perceive as insulting and degrading probably will sound like mere rationalization to the affected subordinates. Managers of subordinates who say they are feeling abused are advised to listen more and attempt to learn more about the impact their behavior has on other people. This sounds simple, but it is not. In order to fully understand one's impact, feedback is necessary, and if the feedback is not given freely, one must directly solicit it. This can be a painful process but is necessary to fully appreciate the impact one has on others.

Subordinates must recognize that, when a manager does something abusive, the action was not necessarily done with malevolent intent. It is easy to infer that if you feel insulted, the boss meant to insult you. Although this may at times be the case, probably far more often the manager intended another effect. It is necessary to seek more information about the message received, which perhaps is not the message sent. Find out more facts before attributing intention to behavior. It's possible the boss simply made a mistake.

However, if the boss continues to make such mistakes, even after being informed nonjudgmentally and with the intent to educate and understand, then chances are there is something else going on. Either this person is so insensitive to his or her own impact that it raises the issue of managerial temperament, or this person is playing power games.

Patterns of Behavior

Abuse rarely manifests itself in an isolated incident. There is usually a pattern of abusive behavior toward subordinates. A manager who is abusive will be abusive on more than one occasion with the same subordinate, and frequently with more than one subordinate. However, in some instances the abuse may be subtle. Sometimes the abuse is identifiable only when whole patterns of behavior are considered. The same behavior may be part of an abusive pattern when exhibited by manager A, but a harmless incident when exhibited by manager B. The difference lies in the meaning attributed to the behavior by the subordinates. If manager B's subordinates feel respected, appreciated, and valued, and do not ordinarily experience abusive behavior from their manager, then they will interpret the incident in question as a temporary aberration (e.g., "She must be having a bad day"). If manager A's subordinates do not feel respected, appreciated, or valued, and regularly experience negative interactions with their manager, they will interpret the same incident as part of the ongoing abuse to which they are subjected daily.

Any one incident of abuse may appear trivial when removed from the context of the regular interactions between a manager and subordinate. Abuse is very difficult to understand if one focuses on only specific, discrete instances. Abused subordinates know this, and it is a primary reason why they may hesitate to report the abuse to anyone else in the organization. Most already have offered examples of their manager's abusive behavior to another manager in the organization, only to be met with a puzzled look and a comment like, "But I've done that too." It is frequently difficult to communicate effectively the subjective experience of abuse at the hands of one's manager, as so much depends on understanding the entire pattern, including, in many cases, nonverbal cues such as tone of voice and meaning attributed to specific statements based on past history. Subordinates of an abusive manager frequently agree among themselves that no one outside the work group could fully understand what it is like to work for that manager. This phenomenon often is demonstrated whenever a new person joins such a work group. The new person is warned repeatedly, both by others outside the group and by the current subordinates, that the manager has a reputation for treating subordinates very badly. The new person may think, "Oh, it can't be all that bad—I've had bad managers before," and accept the new job. If interviewed a month or two later, that very same employee, who had such an optimistic attitude before joining the work group, will say something like, "I didn't believe what I was told before I came here, but now I understand exactly what they were talking about. There were so many red flags, but I didn't pay attention to them. This is worse than I could ever have imagined."

CASE STUDIES: CATEGORIES OF ABUSE IN ORGANIZATIONS

Let's consider a variety of abusive behaviors. As discussed above, in many of these examples, the specific incident may seem rather trivial. Most interactions between subordinate and boss concern rather routine, mundane matters, and abusive interactions may seem like minor incidents. The context of a pattern of such incidents, occurring over a period of time, characterizes a manager's abuse of an employee. In some of the following incidents, it would be difficult to describe the appropriate contextual elements that could clarify the abusive nature of the behavior involved. However, abusive managers likely will demonstrate behaviors falling into most, if not all, of the categories discussed below. One or two incidents do not mean that a manager is abusive. The pattern is what's important.

It is not apparent in many of these examples that the manager was intentionally abusive. In some cases, the manager clearly intended to exert power, and in some of those cases, the intent was to intimidate. In many other examples, the abuse may have been completely unintentional; the manager's behavior may have resulted from his or her own insecurities and attempts to hold things together and appear in control, or the manager may simply have been oblivious to his or her impact. In each of these cases, however, whether or not there was malicious intent by the manager, the impact on the subordinates was negative and contributed to a hostile work environment.

Disrespect and Devaluing the Individual

Behavior can communicate disrespect or devaluation of an employee through either actions or words. Actions may carry this message through subtle means that must be interpreted; words are often very direct in their meaning.

An employee was hired by a company for specific experience and skills that she had demonstrated while with her previous employer. Her first assignment was very similar to a project that she had done in her previous position, and that was instrumental in her being chosen for the job at the new company. Even with this experience, and even though she was a professional greatly respected by professional colleagues in her field throughout the country, her new manager seemed unable to trust her to develop competently a product on her own. At one memorable meeting, he asked her how the project should be structured. In the course of this conversation, he picked up the document that she had produced in her prior job and turned to a section that related specifically to the other company's corporate strategy, which was to expand globally. This particular corporate strategy did not apply to the new company. He asked, "You're not planning to put anything like this in there, are you?" She patiently explained that she intended to include only issues relevant to the company's corporate strategy, so the issue of global expansion would not be relevant and would not be included.

In another example, an employee had just finished a piece of work on a major project. She gave her boss a copy for review. After several weeks, she had not received any feedback from him, but he did route around a copy of a professional journal in which there was an article about the type of project she had just completed. Next to her name on the routing slip was a note from him saying that this was an example of how they should position the project. Since her work actually had accomplished what the article suggested, she interpreted his note as meaning that not only had he not read her work, but also that he assumed she had not included the material or considered its positioning, therefore considering her work inferior. In this case, the manager had intended neither message. However, the employee heard them both, loud and clear. The manager actually was trying to be helpful by pointing out a potential resource for the employee's work, but that was not how it came across. This manager's insensitivity was experienced as abusive by the employee.

An employee was preparing to transfer into a new work group, looking forward to the interesting work he expected to be doing. Before his first day in the group, his new boss gave him some reading material concerning a project on which he would be working. The boss asked the employee to think about the project, and said they would discuss later how to proceed. Motivated to make a good impression and demonstrate his energy and interest in the new job, the employee dove into the project with relish. By the end of his first day on the job, he had produced a document outlining an original and creative framework on how they might approach the project. Since the boss had asked for the employee's ideas, it was a reasonable expectation on the employee's part that the boss would be open to exploring those ideas further. However, a few days later, the employee's document was returned to his mailbox without one positive comment. Instead, the document was filled with critical comments, wording revisions, and remarks indicating total rejection of the employee's thoughts. The employee thought that perhaps he had been off base and had written something inappropriate or naive, so he showed it to some of his peers, all of whom found value in his proposals. The manager may have intended merely to challenge the employee's thinking, without realizing the negative impact of not providing positive feedback on either content or effort. This experience demonstrated to the employee that not only was initiative and original thinking not rewarded by the manager, it actually was discouraged.

An employee was recruited to manage a department. From the beginning, her boss interfered with her performing her duties. She redid everything that the new manager did, countermanded her instructions and assignments to subordinates, and sabotaged her authority with subordinates by directly giving them assignments without telling the new manager that she had done so. Although she had been hired to run the department, her boss would not allow her to do that and essentially turned the job into a secretarial position. Although the new manager had worked previously with people in the organization and was highly respected, the boss attempted to tarnish her professional reputation. After trying unsuccessfully to work things out with her superior, the employee sought help from the Employee Assistance Program and asked for a new reporting relationship. When her boss learned of her request, she redoubled her efforts to sabotage the new manager's career. Seeking legal assistance, the employee finally was able to negotiate a fair severance package. Four months after she left the job, her boss was fired.

Disrespectful and Devaluing Language. A special case of disrespect and devaluation involves verbal harassment. Frequently, this form of abuse will be combined with other kinds of abusive behavior.

The manager of a city park system was verbally abusive to a group of employees working at the swimming pool. These employees were responsible for cleaning the pool and the surrounding area. The manager apparently had little respect for either the people or the task, or both. When making his rounds at the pool, he would call the people vulgar names.

Employees in a small business, all female, were paid to work from 9:00 A.M. to 3:00 P.M. Frequently, at about 2:50 P.M., the owner would demand that the employees stay late, saying there were still things needing to be done. If an employee had an appointment or other plans preventing her from staying, the owner screamed filthy obscenities and made degrading remarks. This behavior would continue for twenty to thirty minutes. Employees were terrified to speak up for fear of losing their jobs. They were not paid for the extra time.

A supervisor in a small, private business constantly criticized the work of an administrative assistant. He stood over her, and at the first sign of her making a mistake, said things like "Should have known you couldn't handle it." He also frequently referred to the fact that she could be fired at any time. Throughout the workday he was rude and loud and used abusive language. Two previous assistants had quit. She stayed because she was in school, and this job was part-time with flexible hours.

Overwork and Devaluation of Personal Life

Heavy workloads have become almost a constant in corporate life. It would be naive to suggest that managers try to avoid overworking their employees. However, the important issue is how the supervisor manages the group, the work, and the people. Supervisors generally assign work to those employees on whom they know they can depend to get the work done, and done well. Therefore, the best employees, or favorites, are even more vulnerable than others to this kind of abuse. For the most part, companies pay managers a salary, so they do not receive overtime pay for working more than a forty-hour week. Employers are supposed to pay nonsalaried workers for their time, although this does not always happen.

Salaried Workers. A division of a large company had a very heavy work load for a considerable period of time, and employees frequently worked twelve-hour days plus weekends with no overtime compensation. Many marriages were undergoing strain, and there had been several divorces. One manager went in to his boss's office to talk about the situation. He said his own marriage was about to dissolve due to the strain caused by his work and the excessive time required. His manager looked him in the eye and said, "Well then, you'll have a lot more time to spend at work now, won't you?"

A large company had identified a group of high-potential managers. These managers were on a special career development program that included departmental sponsorship and developmental assignments. Once a year there was a companywide meeting of all these managers, where officers shared their vision of the company's direction. At one such meeting, specific plans for downsizing the company were discussed. Later in the meeting, this group of managers was told, "You are all on the seven-plus-seven-plus-seven plan—in at seven, out at seven, seven days a week." A more graphic example of values supporting overwork and devaluing personal life hardly could be found. This is an example of such devaluation on an institutional scale. When the institutional values are such, managers who overwork their people and devalue their personal lives are rewarded, thus perpetuating the abuse on an institutional scale.

Nonsalaried Workers. Frequently, demands for overtime work without pay are accompanied by other forms of abuse, as in the example above of the small-business owner who demanded that employees stay late without pay and who verbally harassed them if they refused.

A marrried couple from Poland worked at a university for minimum wage plus room and board in substandard housing. Their supervisor demanded extra night and weekend hours from the husband. He also required the wife to do housekeeping at his house for very little pay. Although exhausted from the excessive hours, the couple did not complain because they were illegal aliens, did not speak English, and were afraid of being deported. Finally, the husband had a heart attack, and they decided to return to Poland. They never had an opportunity to experience "the land of the free."

Harassment through Micromanagement

When a manager insists on overseeing a subordinate's work at a minute level of detail, or attempts to manage the subordinate's time, especially when that subordinate is a talented professional, the subordinate may feel harassed, distrusted, devalued, and incompetent. The various examples below will help to demonstrate how this message comes across and is interpreted by employees.

Micromanaging Work. A manager went on a week's vacation at a time when some important projects were being worked on in the group that reported to him. This was also a time of some anxiety in the company, since a need to reduce the workforce recently had been announced. The manager was in the habit of communicating with his employees by voice mail, and while he was away, not only did he continue to communicate by voice mail, he actually increased the frequency of his messages, as well as personal telephone calls to subordinates. He insisted on detailed status reports several times daily and demanded that his group fax interim reports to him at his hotel. His subordinates were mostly experienced professionals fully capable of working independently, but due to this manager's insecurity, their effectiveness was compromised by his insistence on frequent communications while he was away on vacation. One subordinate who bore the brunt of his panicked requests for status reports was ready to quit by the end of the week, due to the constant harassment to which he was subjected. Even the manager's own boss became frustrated with his anxious interference and left a message for him telling him to leave them all alone.

A manager was unable to view any document without making changes. She sent all paperwork, both important and minor, back to her staff for corrections several times. She frequently changed revisions that she herself had requested (this is a very common pattern). She was also excessively detail oriented regarding follow-up and had a reputation of driving her employees crazy. Because of her micromanagement, everything took twice as long as it should have taken to be accomplished, causing backup in work loads.

A manager left a voice mail message asking an employee to draft a letter that incorporated a list of specific points. The employee was perfectly capable of writing the letter with a minimum of supervision. However, the manager did not stop with listing the specific points he wanted but, without even realizing he was doing so, actually dictated the letter. He treated a talented professional with an advanced degree, who was well respected in his field, like a clerk. This was not an isolated incident of such treatment, and the employee was highly insulted, feeling his manager's continual attempts at micromanagement devalued his competency.

All work done by a benefits authorizer-in-training had to be checked for accuracy by a mentor. Although the mentor's role was to check to see that everything was done according to procedure, he or she could exercise judgment in deciding if an action was correct. The mentor also was responsible for helping trainees understand where they went wrong in processing a case. One mentor concentrated unnecessarily on trivial details and made no attempt to coach trainees on understanding the correct procedures. Her approach was simply to quote procedure, and the trainees had to try to figure out mistakes on their own.

Micromanaging Time. Some managers who tend to overmanage their employees' work will also overmanage their time. Instead of managing by results, they concentrate on how much time is spent in the office. Sometimes these managers actually keep track of when employees arrive at work, when they leave, how much time they take for lunch, and so forth. Interestingly some managers who demonstrate this behavior have never managed large numbers of hourly workers. If they had the behavior would be, if not excusable, at least understandable. If they have never had that experience, the reason they concentrate on micromanaging their subordinates' time frequently is that they do not trust their people. It is a matter of conjecture as to whether they actually are projecting their own untrustworthiness onto their employees; however, their employees frequently are professionals with high internal work ethics and standards.

In many companies, managers and professionals manage their own time. If they have a doctor's appointment or a personal commitment, they just leave. It generally is assumed that the time will get made up, especially since they probably are working more than a forty-hour week with no overtime compensation. In fact, this is considered one of the trade-offs of a professional or managerial job—you can count on working more than the standard work week, but you can take time off for personal needs, as long as you do not abuse the privilege.

Some managers of professionals and technical employees have difficulty with this informal system. In a work group composed of professionals, the manager regularly monitored how much time employees spent at work. Some members had lengthy commutes, and they would frequently come in late and stay late. Their late arrival apparently bothered this manager, although they generally worked more than a forty-hour week, as most professionals and managers do, and the quality of their work could not be faulted. At performance review sessions with these employees, the manager pointed out that he did, in fact, notice that they tended to come in late. He added that he had no problem with their work, and that was why he had not brought it up before, but each of these employees was left wondering why he was bringing it up then. On at least one occasion, he also made remarks to other members of the group about how some people cannot seem to manage to get to work by 8:00 A.M.

A manager sent a voice mail mesage to her subordinates, saying that if they were not in the office by 8:00 A.M., she wanted to know where they were and what they were doing.

Overevaluation and Manipulating Information

Anyone who has spent time in any work situation knows that everyone has some negative characteristics, and everyone makes mistakes. How these characteristics and mistakes are treated depends heavily on biases and preconceptions. In some large organizations, how mistakes are treated may depend on whether the individual is one of a "chosen" group (e.g., a high-potential employee or "golden boy," or someone who has received the highest performance ratings in the past), or even simply on whether people (the boss in particular) like him or her. If the boss likes and is supportive of the individual, then any number of mistakes and negative behaviors can be overlooked. If the boss does not like the person, every mistake and all negative behavior can and will be examined. In smaller companies, especially family-owned businesses, this kind of favoritism is frequently seen. Family members may be forgiven all kinds of grave errors, but if a nonfamily employee, or a family member who is feuding with other members, makes the same mistake, harsh penalties result.

The very same performance can be seen in an extremely positive light or an extremely negative light, depending on one's biases. This creates a situation in which low performers can be protected, and high performers, if they are unfortunate enough to report to someone who does not value them or takes a dislike to them, can be made to appear unqualified and incompetent.

Concentration on Negative Characteristics and Failures. One of an employee's projects was to create a document that was distributed to all managers in the company. The document concerned strategic implications for the company. The project was enormously successful, receiving rave reviews. One high-level manager in the company wrote a very complimentary letter about the project to her boss's boss. The employee learned of this letter only when her boss's boss shared the information with her; her own boss, although he knew about it, never mentioned it to her. Instead, at a performance review after the issuance of the document, her boss brought up some of the early feedback on the project, when it was in a preliminary stage of development. The employee had solicited feedback by presenting a draft to a group of managers. "If it was really so good, they wouldn't have had so many suggestions or revisions," asserted her boss, ignoring the fact that suggestions were exactly what the employee wanted. Moreover, by thus engaging the managers, she was also facilitating their acceptance of the final product.

Employee A completed a major piece of work and gave her manager a copy of the final document. A few weeks later, the manager was talking to someone else in the department who was working on a similar project. However, this other person, employee B, was including a component that was not in the project by employee A. The manager immediately sent a voice mail message to employee A, saying, "It appears we have a serious gap in that you excluded component X." The reality was that component X was relevant to employee B's project, but not to employee A's. In fact, employee A and her manager had discussed previously that this component would not be included because it was not relevant. The manager chose to send this chastising message, rather than a more neutral one inquiring as to the rationale for not including component X (this more neutral message would have implied that there *was* a rationale). By this choice, he not only communicated a lack of faith in his subordinate's ability and judgment, but he also implied that excluding component X was not supported by a rationale and was a stupid oversight. Employee A was infuriated and exasperated upon receiving this message.

Setting Up a Subordinate for Failure. An employee was experiencing some severe interpersonal conflict with his boss. They had some differences of opinion with regard to one particular project on which the employee was working. The boss exacerbated these differences by giving the employee incomplete information and by leaving the employee out of some of the important meetings concerning the project, resulting in a situation in which the boss actually knew more critical information than did the employee.

One Friday afternoon, the employee received a voice mail message from his boss asking him to put together some information about this project for Monday morning, so that he (the boss) could bring it to a meeting. He ended this message with "and we'll see how you do on this." Unfortunately, the employee did not have the relevant information necessary to complete the task successfully—the boss did but neglected to share it with the employee.

Nevertheless, the employee did his best, completed the assignment, and left it in his manager's in-basket early Monday morning. Shortly afterward, the manager stopped at the office briefly before going to the meeting. He apparently did not see the document in his in-basket but failed to stop at the employee's desk to ask about it. Instead, he left the office and immediately called the employee from his car, aggressively asking what happened to it. He went on to say that he had prepared his own material over the weekend and had his secretary come in on Sunday to type it. Although he had asked the employee to have it ready for him Monday morning, apparently he concluded that the employee would not come through with the material when he checked late Friday and it was not there. This behavior also demonstrated a lack of faith in the employee.

While an employee was on vacation, his boss decided that it was necessary to call a meeting of all stakeholders regarding a policy issue. He drafted a letter and sent it to all the parties involved, setting a date for the meeting and explaining the need for them to address the issue. When the employee returned from vacation the boss handed him the project, telling him that he himself may not be able to attend the meeting, so the employee should handle it. The boss neglected to inform the employee about some of the negative feedback he had received in response to his letter. The subordinate learned of it when he attempted to discuss the issues at the meeting. He was met with a fair amount of confusion over the lack of clarity in his boss's letter, as well as hostility directed toward the boss. When he began to explore with the group some of these negative feelings, he discovered that at least one of them had called his boss prior to the meeting to express the very same feelings, yet his boss neglected to inform him of the hostile reception he was likely to get. After listening to the meeting participants and acknowledging the validity of what they were saying, the employee eventually was able to move the discussion away from the group's reaction to the issue and make some progress with the actual policy issue about which the meeting had been called. To make matters worse, after the meeting was over, some of the participants again tried to communicate their frustration to the employee's boss, informing him of the negative feelings that had interfered with discussing the issues at the start of the meeting. The boss later used this information in an attempt to blame the subordinate for the meeting's rocky beginning.

Misrepresenting Feedback about Performance. An employee was in a new sales position. This was his first sales job with the company, and he was highly motivated to succeed. Each week he would call in to his sales manager and tell him what he had accomplished during the week. No matter what he had accomplished, his manager told him about someone else who had done more. If the employee reported, "I made a $50,000 sale to ABC Company," his manager would say, "That's nothing, so-and-so just made a $70,000 sale to XYZ." If the employee set a new sales record, someone else had already broken it. The employee felt that he was not doing well at all and began to worry about keeping his job. He could not sleep at night and developed physical ailments. Still, he kept plugging away, trying to make his manager happy, but the manager continued to brush off his accomplishments with feedback indicating that everyone else was doing better. At the end of the year, the company sent around a list of the top salespeople in the various regions, and the employee was flabbergasted to find himself on the list. In fact, he was the top salesperson in his region.

An employee was accepted for a transfer to a new job in a different department. Her boss gave her the news and then accompanied her to their divisional manager to let him know. After congratulating the employee and saying they would miss her, he then said, "Well, now that you're leaving, I can tell you that I thought you did a wonderful job on the XYZ project." This was a project that the employee had inherited from someone who had been fired, and it was in a shambles when she received it. She managed to pull it together, but it was a very difficult and lengthy project. Many times she had felt discouraged, believing that she was making no progress. Had she known that her managers thought she was handling it well, she would have found that highly motivating; the project might have actually become enjoyable, and she might have performed even better. She appreciated the eventual positive feedback, but it was definitely too little, too late.

In a financial organization a first-line manager reported to a vice-president. For almost a year, the employee was led to believe that his work was satisfactory. The vice-president never brought up or even hinted at any problems in performance. One day short of the end of his one-year probationary period, the employee was discharged. Reasons given ranged from "no reason" to "lack of results." It was later determined that management had decided to change the direction of company goals and wanted to bring in a new person from outside—a person who just happened to be a personal friend of someone in higher management.

Misrepresenting Others' Feedback. A manager told one of her employees that another manager had given her some negative feedback about the employee. The employee did not entirely believe her boss and set out to discover the truth. She approached the other manager and said, "You know, AZ [her boss] gave me some feedback that I didn't understand, and I'd like to clarify it with you if it doesn't put you in an awkward position." She then told the other manager what her boss had said. The other manager said, "Oh, no, that was not my message at all!" and then told the employee exactly what he did say.

On another occasion, this same manager gave this same employee some negative feedback, attributing it to "other people." The employee asked, "Oh? And how many people said that?" Her boss was forced to admit that it was only one person.

An employee, due to some special circumstances of his being hired into the company, was at a higher management level than his peers in the work group. His boss made some mildly threatening statements that he expected the employee to spend more hours on the job due to the employee's higher salary grade. The boss also told him he had been questioned by his own boss and the employee's peers about his higher salary grade. Neither of these statements was credible. First, the employee happened to know that the boss himself was the one who wanted to downgrade the employee's level, because he had said, while interviewing a job candidate, that "there is one person in the group who is at a higher salary grade but he should be at the level of his peers." Second, he also knew that although his peers had approached the boss about the differing salary grades in the group, it was because they felt that all the jobs in the group should be upgraded to the employee's salary grade.

Managing by Threat and Intimidation

Being a manager of people requires skills in influencing people. Yet in many organizations, "people skills" are rarely the primary reason that someone is promoted. Some of these managers find it difficult to accomplish things through other people due to deficient interpersonal skills. Resorting to threats and intimidation is a predictable development under these circumstances. In other instances, managers may have reasonably good influence skills, but pressures in the organization may have intensified enormously. Managers then feel under such stress that they abandon attempts to influence others in favor of coercive tactics. Sometimes, the manager in question is just a nasty person.

A manager had an opening to fill in his group due to an employee going out on maternity leave, and pressure was placed upon him to fill it with an employee he disliked from another department. He agreed to take the employee on a six-month temporary status in his group (although she would remain a permanent employee of the company). After her arrival in the group, the manager prepared a letter for her personnel file that he wanted her to sign. This letter stated that she understood that this was a temporary position being held open for the employee out on maternity leave. Furthermore, the letter stated that if her performance was not "outstanding" during the six-month trial period, she could be a candidate for the company's surplus force management plan (this would result in her not having a job assignment, and being stigmatized as a "poor performer"). The letter further implied a performance problem in her previous position (this was not true; in fact she had received outstanding performance ratings).

The employee confronted the manager by pointing out that the company's leave policy did not guarantee that a person on maternity leave would get the same job back but only a job at the same level. Furthermore, she informed the manager, her performance always had been considered outstanding. She also challenged the manager on why she was being singled out for special treatment, because other people coming into the group were not placed on a temporary status, and such status could not be justified in her case due to performance. Also these others were not required to demonstrate outstanding performance or else be placed on a surplus list. The manager realized that his behavior was way out of line, tore up the letter in front of the employee, and asked her not to tell anyone about it.

A store manager verbally attacked a sales clerk in front of several customers and other employees. The manager accused the clerk of stealing money out of her cash register drawer, and told her that she was not a good employee and was lazy and irresponsible. Later, it was discovered that another department manager had removed the money when the clerk was away. The store manager never apologized to the sales clerk.

A staff meeting was called on short notice. One of the members of the group had a previous lunch engagement with a manager in the organization who served as an informal mentor to him. He told his boss that he intended to attend the meeting until lunch time and then keep his previously scheduled appointment. Within an hour, the boss paid a visit to the other manager, and they talked behind closed doors. At the meeting the next day, when the employee rose to leave, the boss asked him where he was going.

The employee replied that he was going to lunch, as he had previously informed him. The boss then said, in front of the entire work group, that the other manager had come by to see him the day before, and had said that as far as he was concerned, the meeting should be the first priority for the employee rather than their lunch date. The employee was infuriated, because he knew that his boss was lying and because of the humiliating treatment to which he was being subjected. He angrily left, fully expecting that his boss would retaliate against him in some way. His expectation was confirmed.

A manager who tended to have personality conflicts with subordinates was having an especially severe one with a particular subordinate, who resisted the manager's overcontrolling style. Matters worsened, and everyone in the group was aware that there were bitter feelings between the two. During meetings in the manager's office, voices frequently were raised and the manager was seen pounding his fist on his desk. In several of these meetings, the manager attempted to reassert his control with threats such as,

- "Don't make this a personal battle, because you'll lose!"
- "Don't forget who you're talking to."
- "If you don't have this done by Friday, you're through!"
- "Let another manager deal with you—I'm sick of it!"
- "There are other ways of getting out of this group besides transferring!"

One manager whose style was overcontrolling, suspicious, and mistrustful, seemed unable to get beyond this style even when attempting to motivate his subordinates. He either apparently believed that people were motivated by fear, or he just didn't know how to use more positive motivators. At one staff meeting in which he was discussing the group's planned work for the coming year, he made the following statements:

- "We're being asked to do some important work. There's a lot riding on this."
- "There's not a lot of patience in the business—remember what happened to the XYZ team [a project that was disbanded]."
- "We won't be here . . ." (said twice during the meeting).

- "We'll all go down together, or we'll all succeed together" (said twice during the meeting).

An employer hired a manager who turned out to be truly "the boss from hell." He intimidated his employees and brought weapons and drugs to work. He removed the door from an employee's office, saying that he wanted to keep an eye on her. On two occasions, he followed a female employee into the restroom. The employees filed a complaint with the Equal Employment Opportunity Commission (EEOC) but got no satisfaction. EEOC wrote the employer a letter, and the employer wrote back. That was the end of the matter. Management was aware of his outrageous behavior but did nothing. Four years later, action was finally taken against this man, and he was fired.

Stealing Credit and Taking Unfair Advantage

Many insecure managers attempt to steal credit from their subordinates rather than feel confident that their subordinates' successes reflect positively on their management capabilities. Sometimes these managers' behavior in grabbing credit is merely annoying, and sometimes it is obvious to everyone else, including the manager's own boss. At other times, however, this behavior can damage the subordinates' credibility or even their careers. Such behavior is unethical—in another setting, such as academia, it would be considered plagiarism and would be grounds for dismissal or stripping the perpetrator of professional credentials.

A major piece of work had been completed and was to be sent out to all managers in the company. The employee who had done the work had put her name and telephone number on the cover of the document, so that people could call her if they had questions or wanted more copies. Since she had been specifically hired to do this piece of work, she knew that her boss would not dare attempt to put his name on it, rather than hers. However, the boss tried to get her to take her name off the document anyway and put no name on it. He said that, in an earlier instance, something had gone out with the name of someone who subsequently had left the organization, and the telephone number listed was not reassigned to anyone. He said he did not want the same thing to happen, and his reasoning apparently was that it would be better to send something out with no identifying information on it rather than information that might change in the future.

An employee had been working very effectively on a policy issue and was known around the company as the expert on the subject. Now it was time to present the issue to the officers' management group. The employee met with her boss and her boss's boss to plan her presentation strategy. Her boss's boss said that the employee, as the subject expert, should be the one to make the presentation. After the date was set and all was arranged, the employee's boss manipulated the situation so that he would give the presentation himself, telling the employee that his boss agreed with him. The employee, of course, realized what was happening and did not believe that her boss's boss had switched his position, but there was nothing she could do without causing a scene.

A manufacturing foreman was responsible for assigning projects to machinists who did prototype manufacturing. If the project was on time and completed correctly, the manager claimed credit for the accomplishment. If it was not completed adequately or was late, the manager blamed the employees. In one instance, the manager blamed the employees for completing a piece of work late. Later it was discovered that the reported time estimate was actually incorrect, and the work had in fact been completed on time, so the manager changed his story. However, the owner of the business happened to be present at the time and remarked, "You can't have it both ways."

A special kind of stealing of credit occurs when an employer takes unfair advantage of an employee's efforts, or refuses payment after the employee fulfills obligations agreed upon by both parties. Sometimes these situations occur with contractors, not regular employees, but they are still employment relationships. The following situation occurred in a very unusual employment relationship that was transitional between full-time employment and contractor status.

A small engineering company's work load was drying up due to a poor economy. The owner decided to let one engineer go, first cutting him back to half-time. The reason he gave for choosing this particular engineer was that his wife had a good job, and "the other guys are all supporting families." The engineer worked out an arrangement with his boss whereby he would find clients on his own time and, in return for using the office facilities for his independent work, would give his boss a percentage of his earnings on these projects. Later, the boss found it necessary to cut him loose entirely. In the meantime, the engineer had been very successful in finding his own clients, and his work load was quite a bit heavier than those of most of the other people in the office. When his formal employment at the company ended, the boss demanded a much larger cut of his independent earnings. To make matters worse, at a social get-together one of the other employees remarked to the engineer's wife that, since her husband had so many more clients than the other people in the office, he should feel obligated to give them some of his work.

Preventing Access to Opportunities

An employee interviewed for a job that would be a lateral transfer—a job at her current pay grade. At the same time, she was scheduled for two other interviews for jobs that would mean promotions. Due to scheduling conflicts, these other two interviews were delayed for about one week. The manager for the job at her present level asked her in the interview what other jobs she was interviewing for, and she told him. Shortly afterward, her current boss received a call from the interviewing manager, who said that the employee was his first choice candidate, and since he wanted to fill the job as soon as possible, he needed her answer right away. Her boss, looking out for the best interests of her subordinate, tried to buy some time, explaining that she had two interviews scheduled that would be promotions for her, and asked him if he could wait one week. The employee's boss expected him to agree, since there was an implicit rule in the company that a manager never holds an employee back from a promotional opportunity. To her astonishment, this manager became even more insistent that the employee must decide now or lose the slot to the number two candidate. Since the employee had no idea whether one of the other jobs would truly match her interests, or even whether she would be a strong candidate, she was forced to accept the job offered by this manager. He effectively denied her access to an opportunity even before she reported to him.

A management employee was discussing a potential job opening with a friend in the same department. The manager requested a copy of his friend's résumé, so that he could give it to his boss. This boss then mentioned it to the employee's boss. The employee and her boss had discussed her moving to another job numerous times. She was currently in a job that was below her abilities and her management level, and she had been in her current job for more than a year. Instead of continuing to pursue the possibility of moving her to a more appropriate job, he became furious that she had dared to discuss a possible move with anyone other than him. Instead of viewing the situation as normal networking he called her into his office and accused her of going behind his back. He then refused to consider this possible move for her, insisting that she not discuss her career with anyone other than him.

Downgrading an Employee's Capabilities to Justify Downsizing

A supervisor had two clerks reporting to him. Because of a decreasing work load, he needed only one. Both were very good (rated "more than satisfactory"), but he chose one to keep and wrote an appraisal for the other one, rating her "satisfactory." When questioned by his manager, he said that the main problem in her performance was the quantity of work. When his manager asked if the clerk had any control over the quantity, he acknowledged that she did not. He was going to tell her that her performance had slipped as justification for moving her out of the group. In this case the supervisor did not need to do that, as there were procedures already in place for managing surplus that would have enabled the clerk to keep her "more than satisfactory" rating.

Kerr (1988) writes in *Executive Integrity* by S. Srivasta and Associates about the common practice of intentionally distorting performance appraisals for the purpose of justifying current salary action or laying the groundwork for future disciplinary action. He could easily add that the practice is used also to justify involuntary termination, since that is the logical next step as companies downsize more and more. When the beancounters determine how many employees the firm should have, and it is a lower number than the current number, some sort of criteria must be used in determining who goes and who stays. Many companies have tried to use voluntary incentives, sometimes after ranking employees on the basis of performance, so they know where they stand and can make more informed decisions. Sometimes the ranking is done after surplus is declared in organizational units. This strategy is vulnerable to the kind of distortion Kerr is talking about. Subordinates who are the least favored by the boss often are ranked the lowest.

Such a case recently was tried in court, when a former employee of IBM sued the company on the grounds of age discrimination. The employee claimed that he was forced to accept early retirement or suffer an unsatisfactory job rating (Galen 1991). The jury found that IBM had indeed forced the employee out of his job because of age, and the court awarded him a sizable settlement, although it decided against awarding punitive damages (Collingwood 1991; Hayes and Moses 1991). This employee had excelled at IBM for most of his career. He claimed that a new boss passed him over for promotion, saying that he wanted "new, young blood in that job." He further claimed that the boss later raised questions about the employee's performance after moving him to mainframe computers, even though all of his experience at IBM had been with small systems. This case illustrates another common technique of manipulating performance ratings: assigning someone to a job for which they have no training or experience, and then downgrading them for failing to excel. Kerr (1988) mentions managers being advised by legal counsel to refrain from making shifts in responsibilities or work loads aimed at improving an employee's low performance, lest a record of unacceptable behavior be interrupted, removing the legal basis for discipline.

Impulsive and Destructive Behavior

Some managers have trouble controlling their tempers. When a person who has poor impulse control and difficulty tolerating frustration becomes responsible for managing other people, the result can be outrageously abusive behavior.

A manager was trying to avoid phone calls from a particular person who had been calling repeatedly. When his secretary informed him that the person had called again and was waiting on the line, the manager became very angry. He yelled at his secretary and threw a book at her.

An employee was in a meeting with his manager and several other people. The employee disagreed with his boss on several points. After this had happened several times, the manager lost his temper, reached across the table, and grabbed the employee by his collar. He proceeded to verbally abuse the employee, threatening his job.

SUMMARY

Almost everyone who works in an organization has a boss. Human relationships are not always smooth, and this includes relationships where one person must report to another person. But there are aspects of supervisor-subordinate relationships that predispose them to abusive characteristics. Primarily, the degree of power that a superior has over a subordinate can set up a situation for abuse, especially if the organization is one that values hierarchy. Another factor is that many people who have strong power needs are attracted to hierarchical organizations that can provide them with opportunities to exert power and influence. Add to this equation the enormous pressures that companies have been under to become more competitive, and you have a formula for abuse.

This chapter has described a variety of situations in which employees are abused by those with power over them. Some behavior is merely the result of poor management skills. Other behavior is outrageous, even inhuman. In some cases, the behavior may even be the result of mental or emotional dysfunction. All of the incidents described have one thing in common: there are no established mechanisms to deal with the abuse. Avenues of recourse, when they exist, usually are limited to discrimination and sexual harassment; generic abuse generally goes unrecognized and ignored.

The next chapter will examine the more traditional forms of abuse with which companies are beginning to deal effectively. The remainder of this section will then examine both the individual and the situational factors that enable abusive situations to surface in the workplace.

REFERENCES

Bureau of National Affairs (BNA). 1990. *Violence and stress: The work/family connection.* Washington, D.C.: BNA PLUS Research and Special Projects Unit of the Bureau of National Affairs, Inc.

Collingwood, H., ed. 1991. In business this week: IBM is guilty of age discrimination. *Business Week* (November 18): 52.

Galen, M. 1991. Is Big Blue hostile to gray hairs? *Business Week* (October 21): 33–34.

Hayes, A. S. and Moses, J. M. 1991. Law: No punitive damages are awarded in IBM age discrimination case. *Wall Street Journal* (November 8): B2.

Kerr, S. 1988. Integrity in effective leadership. In *Executive Integrity: The Search for High Human Values in Organizational Life*, edited by S. Srivastva and Associates, 122–139. San Francisco: Jossey-Bass.

Lombardo, M. M. and McCall, M. W. 1984. *Coping with an intolerable boss.* Greensboro, N.C.: Center for Creative Leadership.

Strandell, B. 1991. A question of ethics. *Executive Excellence* (January): 15.

Wilson, C. B. 1991. U.S. businesses suffer from workplace trauma. *Personnel Journal* (July): 47–50.

2

Traditional Forms of Abuse

A poll done by the National Law Journal and Lexis reference service found that 51 percent of Americans believe that all or most employers discriminate in hiring or promotions (Karr 1991d). With the passage of legislation forbidding certain kinds of employment discrimination, and with changes in contemporary attitudes, much overt discrimination has been eliminated. Many Americans would like to believe that job discrimination is a thing of the past, and there is a widely held misconception that these forms of discrimination largely have disappeared. However, in many ways the discrimination merely has become more subtle. For instance, instead of being blocked from being hired in the first place, many minorities now find themselves being shut out of important informal communication channels, mentoring experiences, and challenging assignments. Women face similar experiences.

Other discrimination issues face older employees. Corporate America values youth and perceives younger employees as having more energy to devote to company goals. Age bias is a reality and is likely to continue to be for the foreseeable future. And finally, although many companies have explicit policies against sexual harassment, recent surveys have shown that it is still a widespread problem. As with other forms of abuse, employees often are reluctant to report it for fear of retaliation.

ETHNIC AND RACIAL DISCRIMINATION

Barriers to Entry and Advancement

Even with laws forbidding employment discrimination and an increased awareness within corporations and organizations of the need to comply with equal opportunity criteria in employment and advancement, progress in these areas has been spotty. For example, a study by the Urban Institute (Wessel 1991) found that blacks were three times as likely as whites to face discrimination when applying for entry-level jobs. In this experiment, carefully matched pairs of young black and white men were sent to apply for jobs advertised in the help wanted sections of the *Washington Post* and the *Chicago Tribune*. The pairs were matched to be similar in appearance and manner, aside from the racial difference. Each pair memorized similar biographies and practiced interviews to minimize differences. In 20 percent of the cases, the black applicant did not get as far as his equally qualified white counterpart—he either did not get an application form when the white person did, or he did not get an interview or a job offer.

This study also shed some light on reverse discrimination. In only 7 percent of the cases did the black man advance further than his white counterpart. This finding led the researchers to conclude that reverse discrimination is not nearly as widespread as some critics of equal rights policies have claimed.

A report on the glass ceiling by the U.S. Department of Labor issued in August 1991 pointed out how little real success women and minorities have had in advancing into higher management (Karr 1991e). Minorities' advancement has been even slower than women's. Although among ninety-four large employers women comprised 37 percent of employees and minorities 16 percent, the percentages of female and minority managers and executives were much smaller. Only 17 percent of women and 6 percent of minorities held management jobs; only 7 percent of women and 3 percent of minorities were at the executive level.

Many companies are trying to increase the numbers of women and minorities, especially within their management and executive ranks. Some executive search firms reported that the demand for female and minority executives accelerated during 1991 (Karr 1991c), with one firm reporting that more employers wanted to hire women and minorities during that year than in the previous eight years combined. However, a major problem for companies has been to retain talented women and minorities once hired. When minorities perceive that there is relatively little probability of advancement and that they face subtle racial bias at work, there is little incentive for them to stay in such an uncomfortable situation. Attrition rates, especially among minority professionals, have been relatively high. And even though companies are motivated to improve the overall ethnic profile, frequently companies face no penalty if they continually fill the same slots, with a fixed percentage of minority employees coming and going (Gleckman et al. 1991).

It must be recognized that, while the glass ceiling effect is real, it is not necessarily always due to outright discrimination and bias. The Office of Federal Contract Compliance makes the point that often the problem is due more to a lack of training and opportunities to position minorities and women to move upward ("Current update," September 1991). In other words, although there may be no intention to limit opportunities for any group, the impact of inadequately supported programs results in limited opportunities all the same. Once again the difference is between intention and impact. Good intentions are not sufficient; what must be changed is the impact on the affected groups. It may not be enough merely to increase minority recruitment or even to initiate training in managing diversity within the company in order to confront inappropriate prejudices. If these individual changes are not supported by efforts to change systemic policies and practices, improvements in the status of women and minorities in corporations may not be seen.

To retain talented people, companies must understand the difference between intention and impact. From the point of view of the affected individual, it may not matter why the glass ceiling exists. The employee will judge the company's efforts by the perceived impact on him or her. If the employee perceives that the company's intention to improve the situation of minorities and women is sincere, but that a glass ceiling still exists, the employee will be motivated to leave the company in order to find better career opportunities.

Some companies have moved beyond the good intentions kind of affirmative action that merely increases minority representation and begun to examine the impact of internal practices and corporate culture on minority workers. Included among these companies are Monsanto, Corning, and Merck. Monsanto's efforts to increase diversity in its workforce were stimulated by high attrition rates for minorities and women (Ellis 1991). In 1988, 21 percent of the nonunion employees who quit were women and 14 percent minorities. By 1990 these percentages had jumped to 26 percent and 20 percent, respectively. Recognizing that they were hiring large numbers of women and minorities and losing them at an increasing rate, the company decided to find out why. According to exit interviews and focus groups, 100 percent of the departing minority employees said that they wanted more job responsibility, and that they had had difficulty dealing with their supervisors. Furthermore, more minorities than whites felt that the company needed to give employees more help in adjusting to their jobs, and that supervisors' treatment of them was arbitrary and unfair.

The findings from this analysis convinced the CEO that Monsanto had to go beyond affirmative action's emphasis on hiring. The company began a series of managing diversity programs to help participants identify and recognize unspoken biases and stereotypes about race and gender. Not only do employees attend training workshops in managing diversity, but a special program, called the Consulting Pairs program, trains employees throughout the company to serve as in-house consultants on race and gender issues. These employees undergo thirteen days of intensive training and then spend 10 to 20 percent of their time for the next eighteen months helping other employees cope with diversity issues in the workplace.

When Corning noticed that minorities and women were leaving the company at high rates, top management began an integrated effort to change the situation (Hammonds 1991). Recognizing that this attrition costs the company as much as $5 million annually for hiring and training, management began a systemic change effort. It established two companywide teams, led by top executives, to address diversity issues; examined pay and promotion practices; recruited consultants to run training courses on recognizing and accepting differences (required for all salaried employees); established networks of mentors to help new hires learn and advance; and compensated some managers in part on their ability to hire and retain women and minorities. To its credit, Corning did not limit this anlaysis to its internal practices. It also looked outside the company, to address some of the cultural aspects of upstate New York that might make living near the company's corporate headquarters unappealing to minorities.

Corning's efforts in supporting diversity have been relatively successful. Between 1987 and 1990, attrition has declined from 15.3 percent to 11.3 percent for blacks, from 16.2 percent to 7.6 percent for women. The percentage of blacks in management also has increased from 5 to 6.5 percent between 1987 and 1991. In the near future, Corning plans to expand its efforts to attract and retain minorities to include Asians and Hispanics.

Merck, in response to a lawsuit in the mid-1970s, began a concentrated program of affirmative action designed to raise employees' awareness of potential problems in this area ("Current update," August 1991). It began with affirmative action training for managers, who then served as trainers for supervisors, union officers, and eventually all employees. The training made 69 percent of its employee body feel more positive about affirmative action. Merck also addressed its internal practices and policies and made changes where necessary to support its affirmative-action goals. Setting objectives, pay, and promotional practices were all affected. Affirmative action is built into managers' goals. Business units and departments set their own targets, although they may not set quotas in meeting these targets. This causes them to work harder to attract the minority candidates that they want. Managers' bonuses are affected by their success in attracting and retaining women and minorities. Furthermore, a manager's record on bringing qualified minorities and women into the company is a significant criterion in promotion decisions. Due to all of these efforts, Merck has been successful in dramatically increasing the representation of women and minorities in its workforce.

Formal and Informal Communications

Even with companies' efforts to increase diversity in the workplace, attitudes change slowly. Hiring minorities is one thing; helping them succeed is another. One aspect of institutional life that has been resistant to change is the structure of communications. Most learning about how an organization really works takes place informally, with peers or with mentors. Minorities frequently are left out of the important informal networking that occurs among peers, and women and minorities are less likely than white males to have a mentor—a senior person who will help them understand what they need to do to advance.

While legislation and company policies may create the mechanisms for minorities to take advantage of job opportunities by ensuring no bias in the formal communication structure, informal communications are more difficult to change. Frequently, jobs are filled through informal networking. Even when a job is advertised, internally as well as externally, it may be "wired"; that is, the hiring manager may already have a preferred candidate in mind. Advertising the job fulfills the requirements of the formal communications structure, including EEOC requirements. Nevertheless, the job is not truly open.

The old-boy network has not disappeared. As one black vice-president remarked, "The reality of life in America is that if you're white, most of the people you know are white. If someone says to you, 'Do you know anyone for this job?' the people you recommend will probably be white" (Gleckman et al. 1991). This old-boy network is quite powerful not only in ensuring opportunities for its members, but also in taking care of them and helping them succeed. As many observers of organizations have noted, white men tend to feel more comfortable with others who are like them. They therefore choose other white men to work for them and to succeed them. "It isn't any kind of conspiracy," says one noted diversity consultant. "It's because white men feel more comfortable with men who are like them, who have the same character traits, who are aggressive, who are competitive, who can banter, who don't show their feelings when they're disappointed" (Tilove 1991).

Support Networks

One way that minorities have responded to their perception of unequal opportunity in the informal culture within organizations is by forming their own networks. At Avon, for instance, the Black Professionals Association, Avon Hispanic Network, and Avon Asian Network originated as social groups (Keets 1991). They evolved into self-help organizations that encourage minority recruiting and career development. These advocacy groups have become a crucial part of minority relations at Avon, providing valuable input to the CEO, company president, and chair of the company's Diversity Task Force.

Many other companies have similar groups. Sometimes they operate totally independently of the company, and sometimes the company actually encourages such groups to form and provides some kind of support (Solomon 1991). The cooperation between the minority networks and Avon's corporate structure is believed to be responsible for the success of the advocacy groups at Avon.

Some companies go even further in their efforts to contribute to support networks for minorities. Formal mentoring programs have been established at some companies, such as Pacific Bell and Procter & Gamble (Laporte 1991). As part of Pacific Bell's Accelerated Development Process (ADP), talented minority managers receive feedback on their management skills and are given a mentor higher in the organization. Their progress is continually tracked. Procter & Gamble's mentoring program allows each minority manager to be paired with a senior manager of his or her choice. They also have an "on-boarding" program designed to help minorities adjust more quickly to the corporate culture.

As forward-looking as many of these programs and policies are, companies are finding that, in economic hard times, gains in these areas easily can be lost. Corporate restructurings and downsizings often hit minorities hard. When a company downsizes it often targets employees with less seniority, and minorities may be overrepresented in this category. When money and promotions are scarce, it is difficult to meet the goal of increasing minority representation at higher levels. Many companies are currently between a rock and a hard place with regard to workforce demographics: economics drives them to reduce their workforce; however, they also have a commitment to improve their racial and ethnic composition. Since these economic conditions lead to scanty hiring and few promotions, many companies are finding it extremely difficult to satisfy their diversity goals. Since one of the criteria that both attracts and retains minority workers is the probability of advancement for minorities, companies need a much harder sell to attract minorities at the entry level and are finding it difficult to retain talented minorities as well. Without effective and imaginative strategies, many companies could end up in a downward spiral of decreasing representation of minorities in their workforce.

GENDER DISCRIMINATION

Women also face a tough road in the corporate world. Although legislation and consent decrees have prohibited some forms of discrimination and prodded companies to hire more women, the glass ceiling still restricts women's opportunities. However, perceptions vary as to the extent of limitations that women experience; often these perceptions differ along gender lines. Financial World International surveyed male CEOs and female vice-presidents and found the following (Solomon 1990):

- Seventy-one percent of the women believed that there is a glass ceiling for them in financial services; 73 percent of the men believed the glass ceiling did not exist.

- Eighteen percent of the women said that women have the same career opportunities as men; 47 percent of the men believed this.

A poll by *Industry Week* (Walters and Associates 1991) found that:

- Almost 75 percent of women said that the companies they work for pay women less than men for the same or similar jobs; only 26 percent of men said their firms underpay women.

- Thirty-four percent of women said their firm is making a sincere effort to pay equally, compared to 81 percent of men.

Perceptions are one thing; what about reality? When statistics are examined, persistent evidence is found supporting the existence of a glass ceiling, not only for minorities but also for women. In 1990 only 3.6 percent of board directorships and 1.7 percent of corporate officers' positions in Fortune 500 companies were held by women. Only 2 percent of high-level federal government jobs are filled by women. Colleges and universities employ an average of 1.1 women at the rank of dean or above ("Women and Minorities" 1990). Von Glinow, the author of this research, attributes these findings to three general reasons: bias among the dominant group (white males), systemic and structural barriers in organizations, and assumptions that the traits, behaviors, attitudes, and socialization of women (and minorities) make them inappropriate or deficient managers. Older women face even more obstacles than do younger women in the workplace. With age women's earnings increase less, or decline faster, than men's. Promotions are also slower in coming; even in female-dominated careers, men tend to climb more easily. Moreover, job cutbacks hurt older women the most (Karr 1991a).

There has been a recent trend of women leaving the corporate world, fueled in large part by women's perceptions that opportunities remain limited within the corporate structure. Contrary to popular belief, managerial and professional women do not leave corporate life due to work/family conflicts; they tend to leave because of constraints on their career growth and development (Deutsch 1990; Trost 1990). These perceived limitations are causing increasing numbers of women to rethink their career alternatives. Outplacement professionals have reported that it takes longer for a woman than for a man to find a new job after being laid off (Phelps and Mason 1991; Poe and Courter 1991). Many women turn to entrepreneurship after leaving a corporate job rather than seek another corporate job. The trend among women to start their own businesses was one of the most notable changes in the business environment during the 1980s.

Although this is a positive development for women and for the economy in general, this trend represents a serious talent drain for the companies who lose these women. Hopefully these trends will cause more companies to begin a serious analysis of the real opportunities and limitations that women employees face. This should lead to more comprehensive interventions in changing the corporate culture, internal practices, and supporting systems and policies.

AGE DISCRIMINATION

American culture glorifies youth and fears age. Ken Dychtwald documents this fear of aging in his book *The Age Wave* (1989). Among the prevalent myths and negative stereotypes we have about aging are the following:

- People over sixty-five are old.
- Most older people are in poor health.
- Older minds are not as bright as young minds.
- Older people are unproductive.
- Older people are unattractive and sexless.
- Older people are all pretty much the same.

These beliefs about the aging process and about old people, as well as our fear of aging, leads to discrimination against the elderly, which may range from ignoring older people to mistreating and abusing them.

These myths are operable in the workplace as well as in society at large. However, a wealth of research exists that refutes many of the common misconceptions of older workers. Regarding productivity it has been found that:

- Age-related changes in physical ability, cognitive performance, and personality have little effect on workers' productivity, except in the most physically demanding tasks (Goddard 1987).
- Intellectual and creative achievements do not decline with age (Goddard 1987).
- Older workers perform tasks only hundreds of milliseconds slower than younger workers do (Schonborn 1990).
- Older workers can be trained or retrained as well as younger workers can (Goddard 1987; Karr 1991b).
- Older workers show greater judgment, insight, and patience (Goddard 1987).

Regarding the absenteeism of older workers, it has been found that:

- Absenteeism and turnover decrease with age (Goddard 1987; Schonborn 1990; Karr 1991b).
- The work ethic grows stronger with age (Goddard 1987).

Finally, with regard to health, it has been found that:

• Costs for health care for an older worker are less than comparable costs for a younger, married worker with several children. In other words, although older employees incur higher health care costs as individuals, they cost less when considered on a family basis (Schonborn 1990). The bottom line for the company is the cost for the family.

• Rising health costs are not inextricably linked to an aging population. Comparing the United States with other countries yields the surprising result that in other countries with older populations or faster-aging populations, health care costs are much less than in the United States (Winslow 1991).

Workplace Realities

In the workplace, discrimination against older people arises from negative stereotypes of aging and the attendant fear aroused by such images. There is, however, another, very practical consideration: although health care costs can be lower for older employees, in other areas costs can be higher than for younger employees. This situation results because, on the whole, older workers tend to have longer tenure with their current employer (Schonborn 1990), so salaries and benefits are higher. Therefore, quite frequently, replacing an older employee with someone younger can reduce costs for a company. Schonborn cites a Gallup survey that showed an average of fifteen years with the current employer for workers fifty to sixty years old, but an average of only 3.4 years for workers twenty to thirty years old. This difference in tenure results in higher average costs for the older workers.

In an economic environment that drives companies to continually reduce costs, many companies have chosen to do this by reducing their workforce. Many of these cuts have been targeted at the older worker; not only do these workers cost companies more, but by using the right incentives, they can be easier to get off the payroll without resorting to layoffs and firings. These incentives are a combination of age-related and service-related sweeteners. As more corporations reorganized and downsized in the 1980s, the rate of age discrimination complaints multiplied (Miller 1987). In many cases, employees who were terminated or accepted early retirement were replaced by younger employees. Especially if the termination was not entirely voluntary (i.e., if the employee was encouraged to take the offer, was declared surplus, or lost responsibilities even while technically still holding the job), the terminated employee might blame age discrimination and sue his or her former employer.

The Age Discrimination in Employment Act (ADEA) of 1967 was enacted to give older people an equal chance to have a job and hold it. This piece of legislation has been the cornerstone for most age discrimination suits brought against employers. It makes it illegal to discriminate in employment matters (hiring, firing, promotions, retirement, and so forth) on the basis of age. The original act has been amended since 1967; the most notable amendment eliminated the age cap of sixty-five, making it illegal to force people to retire at that age except in certain occupations (Shaffer 1988). The ADEA also has been clarified to include employee benefits by the passage of the Older Workers Benefit Protection Act (OWBPA) of 1990. The OWBPA was enacted to include employee benefit programs under the coverage of the ADEA. This was done to prevent employers from treating older workers differently from younger workers with regard to benefits. It places into law the "equal benefit or equal cost" principle—employers are required to provide older workers with benefits at least equal to those provided for younger workers, unless the employer can prove that the cost of providing an equal benefit is greater for an older worker than for a younger one (Israel and McConnell 1991).

Recent decisions have made it clear that it will be difficult to demonstrate age discrimination when an older employee is forced out as part of a staff reduction. Some courts have held that in industries and professions where pay is closely linked to seniority, firing the highest-paid employees violates the ADEA. However, the Second Circuit Court of Appeals in New York in 1991 held that employers may fire older, highly paid employees to cut costs as long as the dismissals are based only on financial considerations and do not discriminate against older employees as a group ("Current update," August 1991; Murphy, Barlow, and Hatch 1991b). And the Sixth U.S. Circuit Court of Appeals ruled that employers may eliminate positions in the name of economic necessity or efficiency, even when those positions are held by more senior workers, as long as the employer does not act with discriminatory intent (Israel, Sweeney, & Mitchell, 1991). This court, in finding that an employee had failed to present enough evidence to establish that age was a motivating factor in the elimination of his job, also indicated that an employee who is challenging a corporate reorganization or workforce reduction has a heavier burden of proof than an employee who challenges a discharge for other reasons.

On the other hand, in certain circumstances of staff reductions, filling positions with younger workers instead of older workers may constitute age discrimination if the older worker is deemed overqualified for the job. A federal appeals court held that "overqualified" may be "a code word for too old" ("Discrimination cases," 1991; Lambert and Hayes 1991; Murphy, Barlow, and Hatch 1991a). An employee whose job had been eliminated was rejected for thirty-two other positions within the corporation. He was not hired for one of these positions because he was deemed overqualified, and the position was given to a younger employee. The appeals court reversed a lower-court ruling that dismissed the suit.

SEXUAL HARASSMENT

Two forms of sexual harassment are recognized by the law: quid pro quo harassment and hostile work environment harassment. Quid pro quo harassment occurs when employment decisions affecting an individual are made on the basis of submission to or rejection of sexual advances. Some examples of quid pro quo harassment are obvious and easy to identify, but sometimes the harassment is much more subtle (Slovak 1991). The classic example of quid pro quo harassment that is easy to identify is of the supervisor who demands sexual intercourse with the employee while threatening job loss if the employee refuses. However, a more subtle example is when the supervisor promotes an employee who accepts the supervisor's flirtatious behavior in favor of an employee who objects.

The second form of sexual harassment, the hostile work environment, is a much more difficult situation for an employer to control. A hostile work environment can be created and maintained by supervisors or colleagues who create "an atmosphere so infused with unwelcome, sexually oriented conduct that an individual's reasonable comfort or ability to perform is severely affected" (Segal 1990). In order to substantiate a hostile environment claim, a plaintiff must show that the events or conduct complained of not only did occur, but recurred, and that a reasonable person would have found this conduct offensive (Slovak 1991). More recently, a precedent was established that a hostile work environment should be judged according to whether the conduct in question would offend the "reasonable woman" (Hayes 1991). Until then, claims were judged by the "reasonable man" standard—a 154-year legal convention used to evaluate the behavior expected of both men and women. This reasonable man standard still pervades law school texts, although the new standard undoubtedly will affect the wording in new law texts. Perhaps future law students no longer will be taught that reasonable conduct under the law is judged through the eyes of "the man who . . . in the evening pushes the lawn mower in his shirtsleeves" (Hayes 1991).

Although Title VII of the Civil Rights Act of 1964 barred sexual harassment in the workplace, it continues to be a problem. Part of the reason for this is due to the nature of sexual harassment itself; threats of job loss or other employment consequences tend to make victims fear retaliation and therefore decline to take action against their harassers. Twenty-five years after sexual harassment became illegal, surveys find that half or more of women in the workplace have experienced some form of sexual harassment. The *National Law Journal* has reported that two-thirds of female attorneys responding to a questionnaire said that they had been sexually harassed on the job (Slovak 1991), and a Pentagon study of sexual harassment in the military revealed that 64 percent of women had been sexually harassed (Webb 1991). Other studies of the private sector have shown that 30 to 40 percent of women and 14 to 15 percent of men who respond say that they have experienced sexual harassment on the job. The National Association for Female Executives found that 53 percent of its members had been sexually harassed by people with power over their jobs or careers. Furthermore, 64 percent of those experiencing such harassment did not report it, and of those who did more than half said that it was not resolved to their satisfaction (Conte 1991).

Women's fears of suffering negative consequences for reporting instances of sexual harassment are not unfounded. Many women who have come forward have been stigmatized, suffering large financial losses and damaged careers as a result. Observing the consequences for other women causes many victims of harassment to keep silent. In late 1991, the Senate Labor and Human Rights Subcommittee on Employment and Productivity held a hearing on job discrimination, shortly after the Senate Judiciary Committee's confirmation hearings for Judge Clarence Thomas, during which law professor Anita Hill, a former aide to Thomas, testified that he had sexually harassed her. Because of the way Hill had been treated by the Senate Judiciary Committee, three white-collar professional women declined to testify at the job discrimination Senate hearings. They were to testify about their experience hitting a glass ceiling that limited their promotional opportunities, but each of them decided separately that they thought testifying would jeopardize their careers ("Three women," 1991). This incident demonstrates that the negative consequences of coming forward about sexual harassment cause fear of retaliation not just for other victims of sexual harassment but for victims of other kinds of discrimination, harassment, or generic abuse.

SUMMARY

The problems of discrimination in the workplace have not disappeared, although they have changed. Overall, much progress has been made in removing barriers that have kept minorities and women from advancing beyond the lowest-paying jobs. An emphasis on affirmative action and equal employment opportunity has been primarily responsible for the improvements seen so far. However, this affirmative-action emphasis is limited in what it can accomplish in resolving the current problems, which are much more subtle and ingrained in the culture and values of an organization. As Roosevelt Thomas has pointed out, the focus needs to change from one of affirmative action and concentrating on numbers, to managing diversity and concentrating on full use of the talents of every employee (Thomas 1990). To the extent that judgments about people's abilities are affected even partially by perceptions and biases based on race, ethnicity, or gender, the organization loses out by not being able to maximize every individual's contribution. Managing diversity means learning to value the richness that people from a variety of cultural backgrounds bring to the workplace. In the increasingly complex business environment of the future, a company that can effectively harness the diverse talents and abilities represented in its workforce will have a tremendous advantage and will decrease the frequency of employee abuse.

REFERENCES

Conte, C. 1991. Labor letter. *Wall Street Journal* (October 15): A1.

Current update. 1991a. *Human Resource Management News* (August 5): 1.

Current update. 1991b. *Human Resource Management News* (September 9): 1.

Deutsch, C. H. 1990. Professional women seek challenge. *Contra Costa Times* (May 27): 10B.

Discrimination cases warrant attention. 1991. *Human Resource Management News* (February 2): 4.

Dychtwald, K. 1989. *The age wave.* Los Angeles: Jeremy P. Tarcher.

Ellis, J. E. 1991. Monsanto's new challenge: Keeping minority workers. *Business Week* (July 8): 60–61.

Gleckman, H.; Smart, T.; Dwyer, P.; Segal, T.; and Wever, J. 1991. Race in the workplace. *Business Week* (July 8): 50–63.

Goddard, R. W. 1987. How to harness America's gray power. *Personnel Journal* (May): 33–40.

Hammonds, K. H. 1991. Corning's class act: How Jamie Houghton reinvented the company. *Business Week* (May 13): 68–76.

Hayes, A. S. 1991. Courts concede the sexes think in unlike ways. *Wall Street Journal* (May 28): B1.

Israel, D. and McConnell, G. 1991. New law protects older workers. *HR Magazine* (March): 77–78.

Israel, D.; Sweeney, P.; and Mitchell, M. 1991. Reduction in force was not age bias. *HR News* (July 11).

Karr, A. R. 1991a. Labor letter. *Wall Street Journal* (May 14): A1.

————. 1991b. Labor letter. *Wall Street Journal* (May 21): A1.

————. 1991c. Labor letter. *Wall Street Journal* (June 18): A1.

————. 1991d. Labor letter. *Wall Street Journal* (July 17): A1.

————. 1991e. Labor's Martin is out to break "glass ceiling." *Wall Street Journal* (August 9): B1.

Keets, H. 1991. Avon calling—on its troops. *Business Week* (July 8): 53.

Lambert, W. and Hayes, A. S. 1991. "Overqualified" ruling opens the way for lawsuits. *Wall Street Journal* (January 29): B7.

Laporte, S. B. 1991. Twelve companies that do the right thing. *Working Woman* (January): 57–59.

Merck makes affirmative action a reality. 1991. *Human Resource Management News* (August 5): 3–4.

Miller, W. H. 1987. Age discrimination: Industry's new legal nightmare. *Industry Week* (December 14): 49–52.

Murphy, B. S.; Barlow, W. E.; and Hatch, D. D. 1991a. "Overqualified" may mean age bias. *Personnel Journal* (April): 17–19.

————. 1991b. No age discrimination in termination based on salary. *Personnel Journal* (October): 28.

Phelps, S. and Mason, M. 1991. When women lose their jobs. *Personnel Journal* (August): 64–69.

Poe, R. and Courter, C. L. 1991. Fast forward. *Across the Board* (September): 5–6.

Schonborn, B. G. 1990. Fostering the self-esteem of older workers. *Vision/ Action* (September): 16–19.

Segal, J. A. 1990. Safe sex: A workplace oxymoron? *HR Magazine* (June): 175–180.

Shaffer, D. J. 1988. A growing tide of workers claim discrimination. *San Antonio Light* (August 14): 7–9.

Slovak, P. C. 1991. Sex in the workplace: From romance to harassment. *The Human Resources Professional* (Spring): 9–11.

Solomon, C. M. 1991. Networks empower employees. *Personnel Journal* (October): 51–54.

Solomon, J. 1990. Glass ceiling unseen—Unless you hit your head. *Wall Street Journal* (October 18): B1.

Thomas, R. R., Jr. 1990. From affirmative action to affirming diversity. *Harvard Business Review* (March–April): 107–17.

Three women skip senate hearing. *San Francisco Chronicle* (October 24): A3.

Tilove, J. 1991. Managing new diversity. *San Francisco Examiner* (July 14): D1.

Trost, C. 1990. Women managers quit not for family but to advance their corporate climb. *Wall Street Journal* (May 2): B1.

Walters and Associates. 1991. The persistent perception of sex bias. *Behavioral Sciences Newsletter* (February 25): 4.

Webb, S. 1991. Women in armed forces face frequent sexual harassment. *HR News* (March): 16.

Wessel, D. 1991. Racial bias against black job seekers remains pervasive, broad study finds. *Wall Street Journal* (May 15): A8.

Winslow, R. 1991. Health costs. *Wall Street Journal* (July 8): B1.

Women and minorities are still under glass. 1990. *Human Resource Management News* (September 29): 4.

3

The Dynamics of Employee Abuse

This chapter will explore how abuse in the workplace resembles other kinds of abuse. Evidence that abused employees behave very much like other abuse victims will be discussed. Special attention will be placed on environmental circumstances and background characteristics that increase the probability of people behaving abusively, such as increased stress and growing up in a violent or dysfunctional home. Finally, aspects of the organization will be examined for their contribution to supporting employee abuse and ensuring that it remains a hidden problem. This discussion will focus on power in organizations, the importance placed on the hierarchical structure, and cultural values.

SIMILARITIES TO OTHER FORMS OF ABUSE

In one sense, employee abuse is not unique. Abusive relationships abound in our society. Children are abused physically and sexually by parents, relatives, family friends, and sometimes even by their teachers or day care providers. Women are abused by husbands and boyfriends. Elderly parents are abused by their children. One common thread in all abusive relationships is the element of dependency. The abuser controls some important resources in the victim's life, and the victim is therefore dependent on the abuser.

Some people can't understand why a woman stays with an abusive husband. Explanations for this behavior frequently invoke masochistic motivations on the part of the abused woman. The truth is often far simpler.

Many women are dependent financially and emotionally on their abusers. In a common pattern, the husband gradually and progressively limits the wife's social contacts until she is a virtual prisoner in the home, with no means of support and no social network of her own. The abuse escalates gradually. Most abusive husbands begin with verbal abuse, which effectively erodes the wife's self-esteem. The verbal abuse may continue for a long time before physical abuse begins, and the first physical abuse—a pinch, a slap in the face, a shove against a wall—causes no lasting damage, but gradually the physical attacks escalate. By the time they have escalated to the point where her life is in danger, the woman frequently has children, no job, no network outside the home, and very little self-esteem, and she may truly believe that there is no way out of the situation.

Researchers have compared the behavior of battered women to that of hostages (Irving 1991). Like victims who are taken hostage, women link themselves to their captors out of fear that it's the only way to survive. This behavior was first identified as the "Stockholm Syndrome": during a bank holdup in Stockholm in 1973, a bonding occurred between the hostages and their captors. Similar behavior has been identified among victims of concentration camps, Communist prisons, incest, child abuse, cults, pimps, and terrorist groups. Four conditions contribute to the development of this syndrome: a person threatening another's survival, the abuser offering a small kindness, the victim's inability to escape, and the victim's isolation. These four conditions are psychological realities and may or may not actually be objective realities. For instance, the victim of childhood incest is not necessarily threatened with death, but the abuser generally does control important resources in the victim's life. So the victim's subjective experience is one of fear of survival. Objectively, a battered woman can probably escape by leaving the house when her batterer is away, but in her subjective experience, she can see no viable alternative living arrangement or means to support herself and her children. Furthermore, she may fear her abuser's wrath should he find her, which, in her assessment of the situation, is quite likely. Women who do manage to get out of such situations testify to the tremendous courage it takes to escape. In fact, many women do try to escape and fail, which usually leads to more abuse if they are found by their husbands. The dependency issue is a serious one in an abusive relationship.

Child abuse is also a serious problem in this country. In 1981, some 851,000 cases of child abuse were reported (Elias 1986); in 1990 the estimated number of children who were abused was two million (Bureau of National Affairs 1990). It has also been estimated that reported cases may comprise as little as 10 percent of all cases (Magnuson 1983). When considering adults, one estimate is that 25 percent were abused as children (Bureau of National Affairs 1990). Even if a child was not abused himself or herself, observing violence in the family, whether directed at another child or an adult, including the mother, is a powerful influence. Estimates of the frequency of wife battering range in the millions—more than 3.5 million in 1980 alone (Elias 1986), and perhaps six million in 1990 (Bureau of National Affairs 1990). Considering that the FBI believes that marital violence is the most unreported crime in America (Martin 1978), the number of children who observe their mothers being beaten by their fathers may be staggeringly high.[1] A child learns what behavior is appropriate by observing behavior in the family setting. Children who observe or experience abuse learn how to abuse.

Research has established a connection between childhood abuse and abusive behavior toward other family members in adulthood. People who as children observed violence between their parents have been shown to be more likely to become batterers and victims than those who did not observe their parents fighting (Gelles 1972). Adults who learned within their family of origin that violence or abuse is an appropriate way to deal with conflict apparently are predisposed to using abusive tactics in their adult family relationships. What has not been studied is the extent to which a history of having been abused as a child contributes to one's abusive behavior as an adult to others outside the home. Learning abusive tactics might also lead to their use in other situations, such as work. Quite likely, someone who was abused as a child and later abuses his or her spouse or child might also abuse his or her employees. In the work situation the abuse might not be physical, but those who abuse family members physically are usually well versed in other forms of abuse as well, including verbal abuse and manipulation. One estimate is that about 25 percent of managers currently are abusing their employees because they in turn were abused when they were young (Bureau of National Affairs 1990). This is based on estimates that a similar percentage of the general population was abused while growing up. The percentage could go much higher if having observed abuse in the home during childhood is also a predisposing factor for later abusing subordinates, and higher still if children are included who did not necessarily observe physical abuse but did observe mental or emotional abuse, manipulation, and dysfunctional behavior in general. The coping strategies that children learn in the home will be used later in life. If primarily unhealthy coping strategies were learned as a child, the adult will have primarily dysfunctional behavior to draw upon when under stress.

Various profiles of domestic abusers have been developed. Abusers tend to feel weak and powerless, were abused themselves in childhood or witnessed abuse of their mothers by their fathers, cannot tolerate frustration and have a low level of impulse control, and frequently are overly dependent emotionally upon their victim and exhibit excessive jealousy. They frequently display kind of Jekyll-and-Hyde behavior—they appear as a nice person and pillar of the community to the outside world while exercising a form of domestic terrorism at home (Fleming 1979). Employees who are victimized by an abusive boss may recognize this constellation of traits. It is likely that abusers tend to relate the same to significant others in their lives, whether they are spouses, children, or subordinates.

Many managers who generally show positive behavior when relating to others in the work setting will revert to negative or dysfunctional behavioral patterns when under enough stress. Our society trains us well in using coercive techniques to control the behavior of others (this will be discussed in greater detail in Chapter 4). Many people choose to avoid using such strategies, preferring more positive attempts to influence. However, all of us have learned a variety of dysfunctional behaviors simply by virtue of being a member of a society that operates by using punishment and other forms of negative control. Stress can bring out these dysfunctional behavior patterns. Over the last decade the environment in many companies has become increasingly stressful. Competition has intensified, downsizing has increased spans of control, and pressure to do more with fewer resources all have contributed to greater stress experienced by managers. In this environment, stress can bring out abusive behavior not only in those who may have a predisposition, but also in those without such a predisposition. When the demands or pressures become intense enough, most of us are capable of abusive behavior. Chapter 4 will discuss how little external pressure may actually be needed for people to behave abusively toward others.

The subjective experiences of abused employees share some common elements—threat to survival, abuser offering a small kindness, inability to escape, isolation—with the experiences of other abuse victims, as described earlier in this chapter. Employees experience a threat to their survival, although it may not be an explicit threat to their physical survival. They may feel a threat to their job, career, organizational status, professional credibility, financial standing, or any other aspect of their life tied to their work situation. Especially during downsizing or poor economic conditions in society, they may feel unable to escape their situation—either by moving to a new job within the company or by leaving. Also, they tend to feel isolated. These similarities may partially explain why employees fail to leave or report abusive situations. The Senate Judiciary Committee, during the confirmation hearings for Clarence Thomas, did not choose to hear from an expert on sexual harassment. Had it invited such an expert to testify about the behavior of victims of harassment, it might have learned that Anita Hill's behavior in following her mentor to his new post was consistent with the behavior of victims. This victim-as-hostage model is useful in understanding why employee abuse has remained in the closet. The nature of power in organizations contributes the remainder of the explanation.

POWER IN ORGANIZATIONS

Our ambivalence about power was captured by Zaleznick and Kets de Vries (1975) when they wrote, " 'Power' is an ugly word. It connotes dominance and submission, control and acquiescence. . . . Yet it is power, the ability to control and influence others, that provides the basis for the direction of organizations and for the attainment of social goals. Leadership is the exercise of power." Power, like nuclear energy, is morally neutral. It can be used for either good or evil, for increased organizational and individual effectiveness or exploitation of one group at the expense of another.

There is a generally accepted classification of different kinds of social power, delineated by French and Raven (1959). Five different types of social power are described: reward power (controlling resources that could be used to reward), coercive power (controlling resources that could be used to punish), expert power (controlling necessary knowledge or information), reference power (being personally attractive to other people, who are therefore likely to feel a bond or seek a relationship), and legitimate power, or position power (authority vested in a position or role, and accepted by others as appropriate). Kanter (1977) points out that this classification is most useful for understanding the exercise of influence in rather small-scale interpersonal situations and one-on-one exchanges. Large organizations, however, are more complex and therefore also have bases of power that are specifically organizational. A number of systems issues generally determine the relative power of people in organizations. These include, but are not limited to: aspects of a changing business climate that affect the relative importance of different functions, the hierarchy and where one sits relative to the position of the person who must be influenced, whether one is perceived to be on a fast track or have powerful supporters higher up in the organization, and how powerful one's own boss is perceived to be.

These issues affect, and in some cases determine, what behavior is perceived as appropriate. The hierarchical structure of many corporate environments exerts a powerful influence on behavior. This must be understood when considering the elements of employee abuse. In hierarchical organizations, where position power is important, the potential of other kinds of power diminishes. A boss can wield enormous power over subordinates' lives, even with little reference or expert power, because having position power guarantees reward power as well as coercive power. This accounts for another reason why employees are reluctant to report abuse: fear of retaliation.

Neilsen and Gypen (1985) point out that the power the superior holds frequently leads to attempts to manipulate the subordinate and to losing sight that the subordinate has important feelings, not to mention abilities. Furthermore, they state, this manipulation happens because of the structure of the supervisor-subordinate relationship—not because of the personalities of those in a supervising position. In other words, the way that power is distributed in organizations can enable manipulation and abuse. If the corporate culture places great value on hierarchy and does not demonstrate (demonstrate through behavior, not just written or verbal statements) an appreciation of the dignity of the individual, a dangerous situation results. The hierarchical structure of power and the corporate culture together give license to abuse. Furthermore, the hierarchy and the culture collude to give more credibility to the superior than to the subordinate in any dispute over the fairness of treatment. Higher power in the organization equates to greater worthiness, so the accusation of a lower-level person about a higher-level person usually is discounted. Another reason why top management will be unlikely to take the word of a lower-level person over the word of the boss is because, as Fernandez (1987) points out, "top management will assume that if you can successfully take on your boss, you can also successfully take on the corporate hierarchy, and they will never allow that to happen" (p. 89).

Abused employees are in a catch-22 situation. Their harassers are in a position to control a variety of resources, which makes abused employees similar to other victims of abuse. But unlike other victims, they have an added disadvantage. By virtue of their subordinate position, they automatically have less credibility than their supervisors. Charging that they are being treated unfairly by their supervisors would challenge the context of the hierarchical system, which is a very threatening proposition to those who are in a position to help. Even if they succeed in proving an accusation of abuse, abused employees will have identified themselves as whistle blowers, which will undoubtedly cause other potential bosses to question the wisdom of having them as subordinates. If an employee succeeds in winning a fairness dispute with his or her boss, the result is likely to be severely limited career growth within the organization. What has been won?

Employees are well aware of the risks involved in confronting the boss. Those risks contribute heavily to the level of fear experienced by employees. Ryan and Oestreich (1991), in their study of fear in organizations, found that management practice, meaning the behavior of direct supervisors, was by far the largest category of issues that people in organizations are afraid to discuss. A full 49 percent of responses fell in this category, outnumbering any other category by more than four to one. Within management practice, the most-mentioned item was skill in people management, making the boss's interpersonal style the largest single area of undiscussable issues.

It is therefore not surprising that even when employees suffer severe abuse at the hands of their managers, they generally do not make waves about it. This is not to say that it does not affect them. It certainly affects their performance at work; it most probably affects others around them, both at work and at home; and it may also affect their health. The costs to the organization, as well as to the individuals within it, are great.

SUMMARY

This chapter has explored the dynamics of employee abuse, from a psychological point of view and in an organizational context. The dynamics of abuse in the workplace are similar to those of other abusive relationships; just as secrecy characterizes many abusive personal relationships, there is an atmosphere of secrecy around abuse in the workplace. The importance of power in organizations contributes to making the problem undiscussable. The next chapter will explore in more depth how people learn abusive behavior, why tactics of coercion and punishment play such a large role in our behavior toward each other, and what situations are likely to result in abusive behavior being demonstrated.

NOTE

1. Although there are cases of women battering their husbands, about 95 percent of all domestic violence is committed by men (National Committee for the Prevention of Child Abuse, cited in Bureau of National Affairs special report).

REFERENCES

Bureau of National Affairs (BNA). 1990. *Violence and stress: The work/family connection*. Washington, D.C.: BNA PLUS Research and Special Projects Unit of the Bureau of National Affairs, Inc.

Elias, R. 1986. *The politics of victimization: Victims, victimology, and human rights*. New York: Oxford University Press.

Fernandez, J. P. 1987. *Survival in the corporate fishbowl: Making it into upper and middle management*. Lexington, Mass.: D. C. Heath.

Fleming, J. B. 1979. *Stopping wife abuse*. New York: Anchor Books.

French, J. R. P., Jr. and Raven, B. H. 1959. The bases of social power. In *Studies in social power*, edited by D. Cartwright, 150–67. Ann Arbor, Mich.: Institute for Social Research.

Gelles, R. 1972. *The violent home*. Beverly Hills, Calif.: Sage.

Irving, C. 1991. Why battered women stay with abusers. *San Francisco Examiner* (August 18): A-5.

Kanter, R. M. 1977. *Men and women of the corporation*. New York: Basic Books.

Magnuson, E. 1983. Private violence. *Time* (September 5): 19–22.

Martin, D. 1978. Battered women: society's problem. In *The victimization of women*, edited by J. R. Chapman and M. Gates, pp. 111–141. Beverly Hills, Calif.: Sage.

Neilsen, E. H. and Gypen, J. 1985. The subordinate's predicaments. In *The executive dilemma: Handling people problems at work*, edited by E.G.C. Collins, 112–24. New York: John Wiley & Sons.

Ryan, K. D. and Oestreich, D. K. 1991. *Driving fear out of the workplace*. San Francisco: Jossey-Bass.

Zaleznick, A. and Kets de Vries, M.R.F. 1975. *Power and the corporate mind*. Boston: Houghton-Mifflin.

4

Social and Behavioral Aspects of Abusive Relationships

There are at least two factors that influence how we behave with other people: our own personal characteristics, and the characteristics of a situation. We often place much more emphasis on the influence of an individual personality, neglecting strong situational influences. This chapter will look at abusive behavior in the context of compelling situational variables. It will explain how people learn to use punishment in their attempts to control others' behavior, thereby setting up abusive patterns in relationships.

RESEARCH ON OBEDIENCE TO AUTHORITY

Some dramatic examples of ordinary people behaving in a surprisingly abusive manner were demonstrated in two classic experiments. In the first, Stanley Milgram discovered that it was frighteningly easy to get people to deliver what they believed were severe, dangerous electric shocks to other people simply by having an authority figure (a scientist in a lab coat) tell them to continue increasing the pain level (Milgram 1963; 1974). Milgram told volunteers they were part of a learning experiment. A teacher was to deliver electric shocks to a learner in another room for incorrect responses. The teacher could hear the learner, but the learner could not hear the teacher. In reality, no shocks were delivered; the learner had been coached to respond as though he did receive them.

The lab-coated experimenter instructed the volunteer to deliver increasingly severe levels of shock as each session progressed. When the learner began protesting during the lesser shocks, some of the subjects questioned the advisability of continuing. But when the experimenter repeated the instructions to continue increasing the levels, the majority of subjects complied. Even when the learner began screaming in pain and shouting that he had a heart condition, the subjects continued increasing the shock. At a certain level, the learner became nonresponsive. Although Milgram and others, including psychiatrists, college students, and middle-class adults, had believed that most subjects would stop short of delivering what they believed were dangerous electric shocks, the results demonstrated that the opposite happened. Given instructions to continue, more subjects than the predicted "pathological fringe" of 1 to 2 percent (Marcus 1974) continued shocking the learner even though they thought they were causing harm. All of the subjects went beyond the expected stopping point, and almost two-thirds continued to the end, administering the strongest shock on the generator.

In Zimbardo's experiment, a mock prison was set up in the basement of the psychology department at Stanford University. "Emotionally stable, physically healthy, mature, law-abiding" college-age young men were randomly assigned to either a guard or a prisoner role and confined to the prison area (Zimbardo et al. 1973). The local police were even involved in "arresting" the students who were to be the prisoners by pounding on their doors early in the morning and transporting them in police cars in order to provide as authentic an experience as possible.

The experiment was planned to continue for two weeks, but Zimbardo decided to cut it short after only six days. Within a very short time, the two groups assumed their respective roles, behaving as if they truly were violent prisoners and brutal guards. Several incidents caused grave concern about the physical safety and emotional stability of the students, prompting Zimbardo to end the experiment prematurely.

These two experiments tell us several important things about abusive behavior in organizational settings:

- Demands of a role are very effective in controlling behavior.

- People will do shamefully abusive things to other people in deference to the wishes of a perceived authority figure.

- Abusive behavior and behavior in response to being abused may at times have more to do with the roles in which people find themselves than with their own internal personality characteristics (remember, the assignments were random).

• Very little external pressure is needed to elicit abusive behavior toward others.

These experiments are very important in understanding abuse in the workplace—what causes it and what sustains it. Authority is vitally important in most hierarchical situations. In some organizations, rank or level determines everything, to the point that individuals begin truly believing that those at lower levels are less smart, less capable, and generally less worthwhile than those at upper levels. To explain this they point out that if those at lower levels were really any good, they would have gotten promoted by now. In her book *Men and Women of the Corporation*, Rosabeth Moss Kanter (1977) quotes an executive's comment about the organizational culture: "Industrial Supply is a 'Puritan Ethic' company. If you don't make it, you don't deserve it" (p. 29). When such beliefs exist and are reinforced in an organization, abuse of those lower in the hierarchy is a predictable development.

Demands (or perceived demands or desires, or sometimes even wishes or random musings) of higher-level managers can be translated, interpreted, and acted upon in ways that result in abusive behavior and situations. Sometimes the executive whose wishes are being carried out would be surprised or horrified to discover how the request was fulfilled. The powerful research discussed above demonstrates that people are capable of extreme behavior in order to please an authority figure or to conform to the demands of roles in which they are placed. An even more sobering thought is that abusive behavior is learned, and all of us have learned it. The skill of behaving abusively toward others is one we all have in our behavioral repertoires, ready to be tapped when appropriate external pressures crop up.

SOCIAL LEARNING

A behavioral model of social interaction can also help in understanding abuse in the workplace. Such a model, built upon simple but powerful learning principles, yields a parsimonious and relatively nonjudgmental explanation of how abusive behavior is learned and reinforced in social contexts. Furthermore, it offers solutions based on the same simple but powerful learning principles for individuals motivated to change their behavior.

As a first step in understanding abusive behavior, these principles will be explained and how they apply in the work context demonstrated. While it is true that there are determinants of behavior that reside within individuals, this discussion will not focus on them. The preceding discussion of obedience to authority demonstrated that frequently behavior is determined more by the constraints of a situation than by underlying personality variables. How people learn in the context of social situations, and how behavior can be explained by situational constraints will be explored.

Review of Learning Principles

The basic learning principles to be covered in this section are positive reinforcement, punishment, negative reinforcement, and reinforcement schedules. These are not just academic concepts or Machiavellian methods of control. They are laws of behavior that can be used to understand seemingly incomprehensible behavior. We all use these laws every time we attempt to change our own behavior or someone else's, whether we are aware of it or not, whether we use them appropriately or not. Any manager who wants to change behavior needs, first of all, to understand these basic principles.

Positive reinforcement, occurring in conjunction with a specific behavior, increases the probability that the behavior will occur again. A positive reinforcer, then, is anything that, occurring in conjunction with behavior, increases the probability that the behavior will occur again.

This is how organisms (puppies, children, adult humans) learn new skills. An important principle is that the positive reinforcement must be given reasonably close to the time of the behavior that one wants to encourage. Therefore, in order to teach a puppy to sit, a food reward must be given at the moment that the puppy sits. The reward tells the puppy that it has done something right. Similarly, when teaching a child to print, ride a bicycle, or be quiet at appropriate times, reinforcement must occur at the instant when the child performs or has performed the appropriate behavior.

Reinforcements can be anything that the individual values—praise, money, visibility to higher management, challenging projects, time off, and so forth. It is important that the individual value it in order for it to be a reinforcer for that individual. Managers often assume that everyone is motivated (or, alternatively, reinforced) by the same things. They may then concentrate on visibility to higher management as a reward for good work. While some employees may find such visibility reinforcing, others may not, or may even find it aversive.

Punishment is something aversive or undesirable that happens following a specific behavior, decreasing the probability that the behavior will occur again. Again, the subject must perceive the stimulus to be undesirable in order for it to act as a potential punishment.

As will be demonstrated, punishment is the most frequently chosen method in our society for changing behavior. However, using punishment is very tricky. In order for it to be effective, it must coincide with the undesirable behavior. This rarely happens. In most cases, the punishment occurs after the event, sometimes long afterward. Even if the person understands the relationship between the punishment and their behavior, there is nothing they can do at that point to change the prior behavior. The person being punished therefore learns nothing about how to change or improve (Pryor 1984). They may understand very clearly that they are not supposed to do X ever again. This does not mean that they have any idea of what they are supposed to do; even if they know what to do they may not have any idea of *how* to do it, or how to know when they are succeeding. Punishment, or the threat of punishment, does not help the person learn to modify their behavior. Positive reinforcement is needed to teach them those things.

While unwanted behavior may be eliminated by using punishment, frequently this technique backfires. The punishment may stop a different behavior, or may succeed only in inadvertently teaching the individual to be more devious in order to avoid the punishment. It must be emphasized that although punishment might succeed in eliminating certain undesirable behavior, it never succeeds by itself in increasing desirable behavior. Yet people—parents, managers, spouses, teachers, the criminal justice system—persist in using punishment, all the time wondering why those punished do not improve their behavior and frequently making negative attributions concerning their capability or motivations.

Sometimes the goal is merely to remove the offending behavior. In this situation, punishment may work. However, whenever people are in ongoing relationships, such a goal is short-sighted. More often, the manager's true goal is not merely to stop the behavior but also to get some other behavior to occur. This is the motivation needed. The problem is, the manager may not know how to make that happen in an effective manner, or may have incorrect assumptions about the value of punishment as a technique of behavior change or control. (Alternative strategies of behavior control are discussed later.)

Negative reinforcement is not the same as punishment. It occurs when a behavior succeeds in turning off an aversive stimulus. This increases the probability that the behavior will be repeated. The result of negative reinforcement is a state of affairs that is rewarding (reinforcing) to the individual, and by producing the behavior, the individual avoids something perceived to be negative. Closing the door to block out unwanted noise is an example of negative reinforcement.

Negative reinforcement increases the probability of a behavior; punishment decreases the probability of a behavior.

Reinforcement schedules are the frequency with which reinforcements are obtained. When training a new behavior, it is important to reinforce the correct behavior every time it occurs. After the behavior has been learned (when the subject performs the behavior consistently), it is no longer necessary to reinforce the behavior each and every time it occurs. In fact, in order to maintain specific behaviors, it is often desirable to move to a less-frequent schedule of reinforcement.

When the behavior has been learned, the change to a less-frequent schedule must be made gradually. If reinforcement is withdrawn completely, by going from reinforcing every instance to reinforcing every hundredth instance, the subject probably will stop performing the behavior very quickly. After all, the subject had been expecting to be reinforced every time; if suddenly there are no reinforcements, after several tries the subject may decide that there is no point in continuing the behavior or may try some other behavior in order to get the reinforcement. However, if the reinforcement is given, say, every other time the subject performs the behavior, he or she will continue to perform. After a while on this schedule, reinforcements can be moved to every third time, and so forth. While moving to a schedule of less-frequent reinforcements, however, it is important to vary the intervals of reinforcement. If the subject learns the regularity of the schedule, he or she may perform halfheartedly on the trials when there will be no reinforcement. To maintain the behavior the ideal is a completely random schedule of reinforcement. Eventually the subject, never knowing when the reinforcement will come, will perform the behavior perfectly every time. Called *intermittent reinforcement*, this method results in the most effective maintenance of behavior. Behavior maintained by intermittent reinforcement is very difficult to extinguish, or cause to stop completely.

LEARNING THEORY AND REINFORCEMENT IN BEHAVIOR CONTROL

People in social settings are constantly trying to influence the behavior of others. An understanding of learning and reinforcement principles is valuable in understanding the relative effectiveness or ineffectiveness of various strategies of behavior control. Building upon the discussion in

Chapter 3, of how behavior patterns learned as a child in one's family can transfer to the organizational setting in adulthood, a behavioral model of the interactions of couples will be applied to the relationship between boss and subordinate.

In research comparing distressed couples to happy couples, distressed couples tend to use different control strategies in their attempts to influence one another than do happy couples. In the following discussion, *positive control strategies* are those that use, in large measure, positive reinforcement. *Aversive control strategies* use punishment primarily.

Reciprocity is another concept important to understanding the relationships of couples; it refers to the tendency of each person to reward (positive reciprocity) or punish the other (negative reciprocity) at approximately equal rates (Patterson and Reid 1970). *Positive reciprocity* is characteristic of both distressed and nondistressed couples, whereas *negative reciprocity* is characteristic only of distressed couples. In other words, partners tend to reward each other at about the same rate (either high or low), regardless of whether they can be characterized as distressed or nondistressed. However, distressed partners also tend to punish each other at the same rate; this is not necessarily true of happy couples. It appears that in dysfunctional relationships, punishment begets more punishment, at an escalating rate.

Aversive Control Strategies

Jacobson and Margolin (1979) point out that many husbands and wives who fail to deal effectively with conflict use aversive control strategies (i.e., punishment) in their ineffectual attempts to alter each other's behavior. Punishing verbal and nonverbal behavior can be observed frequently in their interactions. These behaviors may include demands, threats, ultimatums, critical remarks, strategic avoidance of eye contact, eye rolling, verbal or nonverbal expressions of disgust, glaring and other such behavior.

Jacobson and Margolin illustrate these strategies in the following example: A wife cooking in the kitchen notices that the garbage is overflowing. She goes into the living room where her husband is relaxing and requests that he please take out the garbage. He responds that he'll do it later. Since she feels that immediate action is necessary, she continues to press and escalates the degree of aversiveness. An escalating exchange of hostile remarks follows, capped off by the wife's ultimate weapon, a threat of no dinner. This finally proves effective; the husband empties the garbage.

This exchange, although somewhat dated, demonstrates the principles described above. The husband, by emptying the garbage, reinforces his wife's use of an aversive control strategy. In fact, he has actually reinforced her gradually escalating use of punishing behaviors. This means she will be more likely to use this kind of strategy in the future to influence his behavior. The husband was negatively reinforced in responding to his wife's threat, since she stopped the stream of aversive verbal demands as soon as he complied. Both partners were reinforced, but at great cost—they became angry with each other and a destructive behavior change strategy has been strengthened. If this is a dysfunctional marriage, chances are he will find a way to punish her later, and another round of aversive control will begin.

Parallels in the Workplace

It is not difficult to replace the husband and wife in the above example with an employee and boss. The situation will be different, of course, but the dynamics would be the same. The boss, like the wife in the example, wants the subordinate to do something. If the subordinate is engaged in another task at the time (perhaps something the manager had specifically requested), and the request is not fulfilled immediately, the manager may escalate the demand in an aversive control spiral, with a similar effect: both parties are reinforced (the boss gains compliance, the subordinate gets the boss off his back by complying), but at great cost to their relationship. They may be angry with one another, the aversive control behavior pattern has been strengthened, and they each may now look for new opportunities to punish each other.

Kanter (1977) documents that this kind of cycle does indeed occur, especially with bosses who are insecure about their own power: "It is a vicious cycle: powerless authority figures who use coercive tactics provoke resistance and aggression, which prompts them to become even more coercive, controlling, and behaviorally restrictive" (p. 190). Moreover, the work situation has an added element not present in the domestic example. In work there truly is an unequal power relationship, in which the boss has far greater power to punish the subordinate than the other way around. If this pattern of aversive control continues, the relationship becomes characterized by employee abuse.

As Jacobson and Margolin (1979) document, the costs of punishment strategies are long-term and insidious. Aversive control strategies tend to multiply over time and tend to be reciprocated. Furthermore, as their use becomes predominant, satisfaction in the relationship plummets.

Why Use Punishment?

If punishment, or aversive control, does not work in changing behavior, and furthermore is so destructive to relationships, why do people—managers included—persist in using it? As Jacobson and Margolin point out, the aversiveness is so compelling that, as a result, short-term changes can be brought about successfully. The pair is reinforced for using such strategies. But what does it mean to say that a particular strategy works in changing behavior? One party gained the other's compliance after repeated insistence; the other gained cessation of the demands—hardly a positive gain for either party. The result clearly fell far short of their expectations.

Punishment resulted in compliance only after a chain of aversive exchanges. It did not result in instant compliance or a harmonious and effective partnership, and is not likely to contribute to such a working relationship. But, because of the short-term gain, the pair settles for this. They may not even be aware that the possibility for a harmonious and effective working relationship is within their power, by abandoning the aversive control strategy and adopting one of positive control.

What the boss probably really wants to reinforce in the subordinate is flexibility, cooperation, and responsiveness. Yet, resorting to punishment when he or she doesn't get them right away has no probability of eliciting flexibility, cooperation, and responsiveness in the future. What is likely to be reinforced is compliance after repeated requests, and angry compliance at that. Moreover, the subordinate is not likely to go over and above the call of duty in satisfying the request. Most likely, the boss will get exactly what he or she asked for—no more, no less. Only positive reinforcement could conceivably result in responsiveness above and beyond the boss's expectations.

There is another reason why people may persist in using punishment even though it rarely works. As Pryor (1984) points out, sometimes the punished behavior stops—if the subject understands what behavior is being punished, if the motivation for the behavior is small, if the fear of future punishment is large, and if the subject can actually control the behavior. Sometimes the punished behavior stops; in other words, using punishment as a technique of behavior control is reinforced intermittently, and intermittent reinforcement is the most effective way of maintaining behavior. Thus, the illusion persists that punishment works.

Two other reasons why using punishment can be reinforcing to the punisher are also offered by Pryor: punishment is often just revenge, and punishment is reinforcing because it demonstrates and helps to maintain dominance. The punisher may not be attempting to get back at the punished individual, but may actually be taking revenge against someone else or against society at large. The classic example of this is the punishing work schedules to which medical students, interns, and residents are subjected. One commonly offered explanation for this dangerous practice is that the doctors in charge were forced to work those hours when they were in medical school, and so they get their revenge by doing the same thing to the students under them.

How does punishment demonstrate or maintain dominance? It can be used in an attempt to force someone to obey one's demands. For example, one manager regularly punishes his employees for going on vacation. He frequently starts this punishment several weeks in advance of the scheduled vacation by assigning new projects, moving up deadlines, demanding more status reports, and setting new deadlines for immediately after the employee's return. He has even on occasion demanded meetings with the employee or requested work done during the scheduled vacation. This manager will use any means at his disposal to get the employee to change or cancel the vacation. It does not matter how long in advance the vacation has been scheduled. In this work group, everyone knows that somehow they become totally indispensable just before their vacation, and they can count on being punished in some way for being away from work. To a large extent, this manager probably is trying to assert his dominance by exerting control over his employees' lives. There may also be an element of revenge in his behavior. Whatever the motive, the result is that the employees feel abused and truly need a vacation after their ordeal.

What is the alternative to this depressing and destructive cycle? The irony is that positive control strategies, if used correctly, are just as effective in changing behavior and result in more satisfying relationships, not to mention more desirable behavior. Managers learn to use aversive control; managers also can learn to replace those strategies with positive control.

Our society rarely demonstrates positive control, since most of its practices in the legal system, child rearing, school rules, and so forth are based on aversive control. People who grow up in this culture generally are punished for inappropriate behavior and seldom are systematically reinforced for appropriate behavior. This pattern starts with parents. On a daily basis, good behavior frequently is taken for granted with no comment, but parents almost always notice and respond to bad behavior with some form of punishment. School systems perpetuate this system of aversive control. Our legal system punishes wrongdoers, but there are no systematic reinforcements for obeying the law—only avoidance of punishment. By the time we become adults, we have learned these techniques well, having seen them modeled on a daily basis. In organizations, where power and dominance are built into the hierarchical structure, managers need to influence others' behavior on a daily basis. Is it any wonder, then, that the manager's automatic first choice of strategy by which to accomplish this is aversive control?

Theory X versus Theory Y

In the management literature there are two opposing systems of belief about how employees can be expected to behave. These were named Theory X and Theory Y by Douglas McGregor (1960). Theory X asserts that employees will attempt to do as little work as possible and therefore must be tightly controlled. Theory Y, on the other hand, is that people are motivated by an intrinsic need for accomplishment and mastery; therefore, managers need only provide opportunities and encouragement, and people naturally will do their best. Another way of characterizing these theories is that Theory X relies on a model of negative behavior control strategies, while Theory Y is built upon a foundation of positive control.

The beliefs upon which these two theories are based predispose one to interpret behavior in different ways. Someone who believes that employees must be tightly controlled and punished for wrongdoing or poor performance will be predisposed to see negative behavior and characteristics in employees. One manager characterized this very common pattern as "managing by exception," or "managing to the lowest common denominator"—dealing with the things that are wrong, under the assumption that "people are no damn good." The managers described in Chapter 1, who concentrate on negative characteristics and failures, are good examples of this type of thinking. This pattern also is demonstrated on an institutional level when policies are written to protect against the possibility of a small minority abusing the system. Relying on aversive control strategies leads to focusing on negative behavior, which leads in turn to concentrating on employees' limitations rather than on their strengths and potential.

However, a manager who uses positive behavior control strategies will be predisposed to see the positive behavior and characteristics of employees. Such a manager will find that employees continually are learning new skills, growing professionally, and demonstrating desirable behavior and characteristics. The manager who uses negative control looks for behavior to punish; the manager who uses positive control looks for behavior to reinforce. Both find what they are looking for, and both begin to believe that is what their employees are capable of. Overreliance on punishment in our society has led to an overabundance of Theory X managers.

Concentration on negative or positive behavior and characteristics therefore has a powerful effect on how the individual is perceived overall as well as on what behavior is elicited from the individual. The same individual might be perceived as mediocre by a manager who focuses on negative characteristics and as a top performer by someone who focuses on positive behavior. In fact, different behavior actually will be shown by the individual, depending on whether the individual is being judged by a Theory X or a Theory Y manager. The Theory Y manager, by using positive reinforcement, will enable the employee to grow and develop into a top performer, because positive reinforcement is necessary for new learning to occur. The Theory X manager, by looking for behavior to punish, accomplishes exactly the opposite. Since punishment is not an effective technique to enable new learning and continuous improvement in performance, employees of a Theory X manager will not be enabled to grow and develop unless they can manage to find positive reinforcement elsewhere. Also, their manager is unlikely to perceive them in a positive light. Both types of expectations become self-fulfilling prophecies.

The impact of such self-fulfilling prophecies is enormous in terms of employee capability, individual performance, and organizational success. The prevalence of Theory X philosophy and behavior can be explained by the simple laws of learning demonstrated in this chapter. To move to Theory Y requires a conscious effort, but certainly not a magical one. All it takes is learning and applying the basic principles of behavior. Becoming conscious of an ineffective strategy is the first step in changing it. Perhaps understanding some of the behavioral laws that account for the persistence of punishment can help managers abandon it for more effective strategies.

SUMMARY

This chapter has demonstrated that in order to understand the nature of abuse in the workplace, some very basic principles of behavior and learning need to be understood. Specifically, managers need to become more knowledgeable in analyzing situational influences on behavior and in using positive reinforcement rather than punishment in interactions. Managers also need to be extremely sensitive to the powerful influence of authority, in light of the fact that all people have the capacity to behave abusively toward others.

Coercive methods of influencing other people are experienced as abusive and contribute to ineffective influence attempts, while positive reinforcement is experienced as enabling and results in effectively influencing others. The power of the learning principles discussed in this chapter is in their potential for developing positive influence skills.

REFERENCES

Jacobson, N. S. and Margolin, G. 1979. *Marital therapy: Strategies based on social learning and behavior exchange principles*. New York: Brunner/Mazel.

Kanter, R. M. 1977. *Men and women of the corporation*. New York: Basic Books.

McGregor, D. 1960. *The human side of enterprise*. New York: McGraw-Hill.

Marcus, S. 1974. Review of *Obedience to authority: An experimental view. New York Times* (January 13): Sec. 7, 1–3.

Milgram, S. 1963. Behavioral study of obedience. *Journal of Abnormal and Social Psychology* 67(4): 371–78.

——— . 1974. *Obedience to authority: An experimental view*. New York: Harper & Row.

Patterson, G. R. and Reid, J. B. 1970. Reciprocity and coercion: Two facets of social systems. In *Behavior modification in clinical psychology*, edited by C. Neuringer and J. L. Michael, 133–77. New York: Appleton-Century-Crofts.

Pryor, K. 1984. *Don't shoot the dog! The new art of teaching and training*. New York: Bantam Books.

Zimbardo, P. G.; Banks, W. C.; Haney, C.; and Jaffe, D. 1973. The mind is a formidable jailer: A Pirandellian prison. *New York Times Magazine* (April 8): 38–60.

Part II
Institutional Abuse

As distasteful as some of the examples of employee abuse described in Part 1 are, it is unfortunately not a problem limited to some bosses and some subordinates. Aspects of the corporate culture in many organizations support, if not encourage, employee abuse. Some corporate policies, such as substance abuse policies, and some management practices, such as the use of personality tests for team-building purposes, can result in abusive behavior and situations if not supported by strong respect for the individual. This section explores the potential for employee abuse on a larger scale.

Chapter 5 looks at employee treatment in the context of ethics and explores how ethical issues faced by managers frequently revolve around fair treatment of employees. Chapter 6 examines the elements of corporate culture that contribute to workaholism and overwork. The relationship of workaholism to loss of productivity is also explored. Chapter 7 considers some specific policies, procedures, and practices that usually are directed toward cost reduction. Although the organizations do not undertake these actions with the intent to abuse or harass, frequently that is the impact. Chapters 8 and 9 catalog a variety of new developments in employee testing and privacy issues that potentially may contribute to a hostile work environment.

5

The Ethics of Employee Treatment

Many companies have statements in their corporate strategies or values to the effect that "people are our most important resource." Many employees are skeptical about such statements because they do not see this value lived up to in the organization's daily life. Such statements, if they are not to become empty words, need to be reinforced by other consistent value messages, and behavior that supports those values needs to be reinforced by the organization.

CORPORATE ETHICS

There has been an explosion of interest in business ethics within American corporations in the last decade. Public scandals concerning highly visible ethical lapses in corporations have contributed to an increased awareness of the importance of ethical behavior. The accelerating rate of change in the business world also has played a part in a new willingness to examine ethical values and standards. Some skeptics attribute the increased interest in business ethics to the expectation that tough new federal sentencing guidelines would be enacted (Anand 1991). These guidelines, which took effect on November 1, 1991, increase fines for corporate crimes. At the same time, they encourage judges to apply more lenient punishments for legal and regulatory violations if a company can demonstrate that it has committed substantial resources to programs that encourage ethical behavior (Feder 1991).

One result of this increasing concentration on corporate ethics has been the adoption of codes of ethics. In 1985, a survey of three hundred large U.S. companies conducted by Bentley College's Center for Business Ethics found that 75 percent had formal codes of ethics. When the survey was repeated in 1990, 91 percent had incorporated codes of ethics (Edwards and Bennett 1987; Anand 1991). However, far fewer companies have other support structures to ensure that their codes of ethics are institutionalized. In 1985, less than 15 percent of companies had ethics committees, only about 5 percent had ethical ombudsmen, and only three companies had ethics judiciary boards (Hoffman 1989). These numbers are increasing as well. According to the Ethics Resource Center, currently more than 15 percent of companies employing fifty thousand or more people have established ethics offices—almost all within the last five years (Feder 1991). These trends illustrate the increasing corporate emphasis on ethics, but there is disagreement as to whether these types of supporting programs help build a strong ethical culture. Companies such as Johnson & Johnson, for instance, have a culture in which ethical values are the basic building block for all management decisions. It has accomplished this without an ethics office, although it does have a credo that stresses ethical behavior. Its culture has enabled all employees to internalize the values expressed in the credo.

The relationship of a code of ethics to an ethical culture is by no means direct. Data indicate that there is little relationship between codes of conduct and illegal behavior of corporations (Mathews 1987). William Frederick (quoted in Wartzman 1987) says this happens because typically codes emphasize improving corporate balance sheets. He cites a number of studies that show that even the most honest people are apt to become dishonest and unmindful of their civic responsibilities when placed in a typical corporate environment, and claims the culprit for this phenomenon is a business climate that condones wrongdoing for the company's benefit. Frederick cites studies supporting this view. In one, 91 percent of U.S. managers considered trust to be important, but only 12 percent thought it could help achieve career success. Ambition was thought to be important by 75 percent, and 73 percent also believed it could help them be successful. In another study, researchers found that 70 percent of executives and middle managers experienced pressure to conform to organizational standards that often caused them to compromise personal principles.

Did these managers and executives simply have weak moral standards to start with? This is not likely. When managers are asked about the values and personal attributes to which they aspire, their responses are very similar to those of other people. There are a variety of social and behavioral reasons why people might behave in ways that contradict their own deeply held values (see Chapter 4), including perceived pressure or demands from above, and what kinds of behavior are rewarded. These are all aspects of the corporate culture. If managers and employees perceive increased pressure to "make the numbers," they may conclude rightly that higher management does not really care how they do it—and in fact does not want to know—and will look away to avoid dealing with how it's getting done (Gellerman 1986). If management ignores the existence of certain activities discouraged by the company's code of ethics, a clear message is sent to the organization that such behavior is tolerated or even condoned.

Subjects stressed by corporate codes of ethics also shed some light on the question of what behavior the corporate culture supports. Although codes of ethics presumably are designed to prevent wrongdoing, Mathews (1987) found that 75 percent of Fortune 500 companies' codes failed to address: the firm's role in civic, community, and environmental affairs; consumer relations; product quality; product safety; and worker health and safety. However, about 75 percent do deal with conflicts of interest. Employee conduct in general is the most widely covered topic. In a survey by the Conference Board, more than 90 percent of companies identified the three major areas of ethical problems as: employee conflicts of interest, employees' acceptance of inappropriate gifts, and sexual harassment (Walters 1987). According to Mathews (1987), codes of ethics focus on infractions against the corporation or on specific illegal activity on behalf of the firm (such as bribery), rather than on issues directly related to consumers and the general public (like the environment or product safety and quality). Looking at the data another way, companies seem more concerned about employees' conduct against the firm than they are about the firm's conduct against employees, customers, and the general public.

CODES OF ETHICS VERSUS CODES OF CONDUCT

To understand why this is so, note that employee codes of conduct have existed in many companies longer than have codes of ethics. With the new emphasis on ethics, some codes of conduct now are called codes of ethics. In the business literature, generally no distinction is made between codes of ethics or codes of conduct. In any case, these codes still deal mainly with employee conduct and for the most part have not evolved to the point of addressing ethical issues on an institutional or cultural basis. As long as the confusion exists between a code of ethics and a code of conduct, most codes of ethics likely will be merely restatements of the issues generally covered in codes of conduct, which exist mainly to protect the corporation from the undesirable behavior of employees.

This point is important when considering what effect the corporate culture has on how employees are treated. Two issues are relevant: what the codes say directly about treatment of employees, and what is communicated indirectly by what the culture actually supports.

ETHICAL ISSUES MANAGERS FACE DAILY

Very few of the areas covered by codes of ethics deal with how the company, through management, deals with employees. Yet, most managers will run up against this area of ethical issues far more frequently than any other. The most visible and spectacular abuses of ethics may concern questionable financial transactions and customers being cheated and misled. However, the most frequent abuses probably occur in the realm of how employees are treated on a daily basis by their supervisors and by their companies. Strandell (1991) maintains that thousands of managers victimize their employees every day, contributing to the stress and unhappiness of millions of corporate workers. In fact, many managers will find themselves facing dilemmas regarding fair treatment of employees almost every day, and many of these situations will have ethical components, whether or not the manager realizes it at the time.

Barbara Ley Toffler (1986) describes a study in which managers were asked to describe situations in which they had been involved and that they felt had an ethical component. The incidents described fell into three main categories: managing human resource processes and personnel, managing external constituents, and managing personal risk versus company loyalty. Two-thirds of the incidents described fell into the first category, demonstrating that managers think that the way the organization deals with employees is a legitimate ethical concern. The issues involved dealt most frequently with performance evaluation and resultant hiring, firing, promotion, and demotion decisions; designing and administering personnel policies and systems, such as disability policies and reward systems; and managing relationships on the job.

The experience of one of the Baby Bells in establishing an ethics office confirms that employees consider fair treatment an ethical issue. Of the confidential calls coming to NYNEX's newly established ethics hotline, 42 percent involved personnel issues such as the fairness of a supervisor or promotion procedures (Feder 1991). NYNEX found this surprising at first, until it checked with other companies. Other evidence that everyday ethical issues primarily concern fairness of employee treatment comes from the Corporate Ombudsman Association. The types of cases most frequently handled by Ombudsmen's offices in the private sector are: hierarchical conflicts (supervisor-subordinate tensions), performance evaluation, promotion, termination, salaries and benefits, general "mean-ness" (all types of harassment) and psychological problems, and transfer and work assignments (Ziegenfuss et al. 1989).

There appear to be major discontinuities between the ethical issues identified by companies and included in written codes of ethics and conduct, and the ethical issues with which managers and employees struggle daily. This may be one reason why ethics and conduct codes are often not well received. The previously mentioned Conference Board survey identified two problems with such codes: employees frequently perceive their tone to be accusatory, indicating that employees are not trusted, or they consider them to be merely rhetoric (Walters and As-sociates 1987).

Another reason for the poor reception among employees may be the previously cited confusion between codes of ethics and codes of conduct. Although the difference between the two may not be explicit in their minds, employees expect that a code of ethics will cover more of the issues associated with higher ethical principles, such as protecting the com-munity and individuals (including employees) from abuses on behalf of the corporation. Then, when a new code is introduced into the organization but covers mainly the topics covered by a traditional code of conduct, serving to protect the corporation from abuses by its own workers, employees become disillusioned. Hoffman (1989) finds distressing that in the previously cited survey of Fortune 500 companies, of the 20 percent of companies that had made structural or governance changes in order to institutionalize ethics, only 7 percent had introduced an employee bill of rights. This amounts to 1.4 percent of the entire sample. Employees apparently find this distressing as well.

Most articles on improving corporate ethics neglect the important area of how the organization and its managers deal with employees. Unless top executives concentrate more on the ethics of how employees are treated, their implementation of codes of conduct, ethics training, and so forth will be for naught, because employees judge the ethics of their role models by the way they are treated by those role models. If employees perceive that they are being abused by top management, their own supervisor, or management practices, attempts to train them in customer orientation and ethical behavior in the marketplace will have little credibility.

CONSISTENCY BETWEEN STATED VALUES AND BEHAVIOR

As mentioned before, having a code of ethics by no means guarantees that a company will have an ethical culture. Many other components must be involved in creating a strong ethical culture, including support structures to ensure the institutionalization of ethics (e.g., ombudsmen, ethics committees, ethics judiciary boards), strong ethical values, rewards (or at least no punishment) for behaving consistently with the company's values and stated principles, and perhaps most importantly, behavior consistent with values regarding the dignity of the individual.

Abused employees are far more likely to abuse customers and other stakeholders. They are also more likely to be cynical about the organization's ethical values and therefore may be inclined to take advantage of their employer when the situation arises. Some research evidence shows that when employees feel unfairly treated by their employer, they are more likely to act against the organization as a way to balance the perceived inequity (Greenberg 1990; Hollinger and Clark 1983). On the positive side, when employees view their company's human resource policies favorably (and presumably feel treated fairly), customers have a favorable perception of the quality of service they receive (Goddard 1989). Common sense as well as a growing body of research tells us that fair treatment of employees will affect not only employees' ethical behavior but also the public's perception of the company and its ethics.

The most important factor in whether employees feel treated fairly is what values employees perceive are being lived up to in the daily behavior of its managers—not whether the company has created written statements attesting to the value of people and the dignity of the individual. As with customers, perception is everything. If the customer feels mistreated, there will be a negative impact on the company. Many companies that have embraced this concept with regard to their customers have not yet accepted that it is equally valid with regard to employees. Does this mean that managers have to pander to employees, treat them with kid gloves, give them everything they want? No, of course not, no more than customer satisfaction means giving customers everything they want no matter what the cost. It is possible to satisfy the customer by negotiating a fair deal. The same is possible with employees. What's important is fairly considering the needs of the customer or employee and treating each with respect and dignity.

In order to do this, it is useful to borrow another concept from the customer satisfaction terminology. Several service companies that are recognized as superior service providers (e.g., Federal Express, SAS) have incorporated into their value system the concept that every time an employee interacts with a customer or potential customer, it is an opportunity to either delight the customer or to ruin the customer's perception of the company. SAS refers to these contacts as "moments of truth." If the customer is delighted, he or she will come back. If the customer feels badly treated, not only will the customer's perception of the company be affected but the perceptions of many other people as well, since a dissatisfied customer generally will tell many other people about the incident. This idea that every interaction has the potential for enormous cost or benefit applies to the ethics of employee treatment. Strong corporate beliefs concerning the value of employees as individuals can be used to create an ethic of fair employee treatment. In this view, managers can be encouraged to view every contact with an employee as an opportunity to either strengthen the corporate culture and reinforce productivity, success, and motivation, or to lose the hearts and minds of employees and thus destroy their desire to help the company succeed.

Some companies have taken this value even further. One of Federal Express's corporate principles is "Customer satisfaction starts with employee satisfaction." But Federal Express does not stop with a value statement. It has a variety of mechanisms, including its Guaranteed Fair Treatment Procedure, to ensure that employee opinions are heard ("Federal Express Review Process" 1991). If employees have grievances, they have several channels of appeal. The first is management review. The grievance goes to a team consisting of a manager, a senior manager, and a managing director. If the employee is not satisfied within seven days with the resolution, he or she can take the grievance to the level of office review. A vice-president and a senior vice-president review the grievance at this stage. Again, if the grievance is not satisfied to the employee's satisfaction, it goes to executive review. The CEO, COO, CFO and two senior vice-presidents then review the grievance. This group spends at least part of one day per week reviewing the cases that come to them. In no other company of its size do the top officers spend so much of their time on employee grievances. That they do provides tangible evidence of the value placed on the people in the organization. Federal Express, which won the Malcolm Baldridge Award for service quality in 1990, attributes a great deal of its success to its fair treatment of employees. The COO of Federal Express has stated that the Guaranteed Fair Treatment Procedure brings poor managers to the attention of top management very quickly. By so doing, the company can initiate corrective action so that employees can continue to feel empowered to perform to the best of their ability. It seems to work: the Malcolm Baldridge judges found that 91 percent of Federal Express employees are satisfied.

Rosenbluth (1991) explained how he crafted a hugely successful travel and information business by putting employees ahead of customers. The values by which Rosenbluth Travel operates are simple. There is a hierarchy of concerns: people, service, profits. Upper management believes that "only if our people are first in our eyes will they be able to put the customer first in theirs." Upper management focuses on the people in the organization, the people focus on service, and profits result. Rosenbluth believes that profits are truly a by-product of putting the employees (they like to call them "associates") ahead of their customers. Most companies reverse the order of these three concerns then wonder why they cannot get all three values to support each other.

SUMMARY

Companies that demonstrate the great value they place on their employees create strong corporate cultures. Employees find it easy to behave in the best interests of their customers and their companies. These companies are not likely to adopt policies that might be abusive, and managers are not likely to use policies and management practices in abusive ways. However, human beings being human, circumstances will arise even in the best of companies that may cause employees to question the fairness of how they are treated. That there are avenues of recourse and mechanisms available to correct the situations is what makes these companies exemplary in the fair and equitable treatment of employees. It is not a coincidence that companies that win service and quality awards are the same ones that emphasize the ethics of employee treatment.

REFERENCES

Anand, V. 1991. A new emphasis on ethics is catching on in business. *Investors Daily* (October 10): 10.

Business Roundtable. 1988. The rationale for ethical corporate behavior. *Business and Society Review* (Winter): 33–36.

Edwards, G. and Bennett, K. 1987. Ethics and HR standards in practice. *Personnel Administrator* (December): 62–66.

Feder, B. J. 1991. Helping corporate America hew to the straight and narrow. *New York Times* (November 3): F5.

Federal Express review process. 1991. *Human Resource Management News* (June 17): 2–3.

Gellerman, S. W. 1986. Why "good" managers make bad ethical choices. *Harvard Business Review* (July-August): 85–90.

Goddard, R. W. 1989. Corporate America's moral change. *Personnel Journal* (October): 30–37.

Greenberg, J. 1990. Employee theft as a reaction to underpayment inequity: The hidden cost of pay cuts. *Journal of Applied Psychology* 75 (5): 561–68.

Hoffman, W. M. 1989. The cost of a corporate conscience. *Business and Society Review* (Spring): 46–47.

Hollinger, R. D. and Clark, J. P. 1983. *Theft by employees*. Lexington, Mass.: Lexington Books.

Mathews, M. C. 1987. Codes of ethics: Organizational behavior and misbehavior. In *Research in corporate social performance and policy*, edited by W. C. Frederick and L. E. Preston, vol. 9, 107–30. Greenwich, Conn.: JAI Press.

Rosenbluth, H. 1991. Tales from a nonconformist company. *Harvard Business Review* (July–August): 26–36.

Strandell, B. 1991. A question of ethics. *Executive Excellence* (January): 15.

Toffler, B. L. 1986. *Tough choices: Managers talk ethics*. New York: John Wiley & Sons.

Walters and Associates. 1987. Ethics codes get a mixed reception. *Behavioral Sciences Newsletter* (October 12): 2.

Wartzman, R. 1987. Nature or nurture? Study blames ethical lapses on corporate goals. *Wall Street Journal* (October 9): B1.

Ziegenfuss, J. T. Jr.; Rowe, M.; Robbins, L.; and Munzenrider, R. 1989. Corporate ombudsmen. *Personnel Journal* (March): 76–79.

6

Overwork and the Workaholic Organization

Workaholism used to be an idiosyncratic behavior. People would either chuckle admiringly or shake their heads with pity when describing someone as a workaholic, depending on what they perceived to be the costs to the individual involved. In recent years, with the onslaught of intensified competition, workaholism or overwork has become the cultural norm in many organizations. In such a circumstance, the disorder can move beyond the realm of individual psychopathology and into the realm of employee abuse.

EFFECTS ON EMPLOYEES

In this country, overwork is becoming a frequent workplace hazard. With the successive waves of downsizings that many companies have experienced, there are simply fewer people to do the work unless the work is restructured or reduced (and in most cases it's not). In many organizations there may not be a formal downsizing, but other techniques may be used to avoid adding to personnel: not replacing employees who leave or not adding to staff as workloads grow. This situation has become so common in organization life that new terms have been coined to describe it: job engorgement, or the job redesign strategy for the 1990s ("Job Engorgement" 1991).

More Time at Work

Recent surveys have shown that employees are working more hours. Among managers, one 1990 survey found that 24 percent spend forty-nine hours or more per week on the job; another found that 57 percent worked six to twenty hours beyond the forty-hour week, and 95 percent work more than forty hours per week (Kilborn 1990). These studies found that not only were more people working longer hours than ten years before, but the hours worked were 20 percent longer. Furthermore, 66 percent of managers in one of the studies felt under more stress than they had felt ten years before.

Among nonsalaried employees, factory workers are putting in almost four hours of overtime per week, the most in nearly twenty years (Kilborn 1990). In the steel industry, where overtime has become the norm (Ansberry 1989), union laborers worked nearly twice as many overtime hours in the late 1980s as they did between 1981 and 1985. This overtime is blamed by many for the increase in work-related injuries and disabilities. Permanent work-related disabilities jumped 16 percent between 1986 and 1987—from sixty thousand to seventy thousand (Ansberry 1989). This jump cannot be attributed to an increase in the absolute number of workers: for every one hundred workers, the number of job-related injuries and illnesses increased 5 percent in 1987 (in manufacturing, the increase was 12 percent). Safety and labor officials have tied the injury-rate rise to the effects of mergers and competition. Smaller work crews, overtime, faster assembly lines, and the unrelenting drive to produce are seen as causes. A recent University of Texas study cited more overtime and employee turnover as triggering 93 percent of the injuries it examined (Ansberry 1989).

Executives also are working more hours. According to a 1985 survey by Korn/Ferry International, the typical Fortune 500 or Service 500 respondent reported working an average of fifty-six hours per week (three hours more than in 1979). Use of vacation time was down too—the average was fourteen days, down from sixteen in 1979 (Worthy 1987). Another survey done by Heidrick and Struggles found that 60 percent of CEOs were working more than sixty hours per week in 1984, compared with 44 percent in 1980. By 1990, 70 percent of CEOs were putting in sixty or more hours per week (Solo 1990).

Pressure and Demands on Personal Time

In addition to overwork itself, another factor that must be considered is the environment of threat and uncertainty that causes such overwhelming pressures to produce. One psychologist who treats corporate clients said, in 1988, "They were pushing people at an extraordinary pace. They were working until 10 p.m., working weekends. The feeling was that if they didn't do it, they'd lose their jobs. Who can live every day like that?" (Bennett 1988).

Ironically, in the few years since then managers in many industries say that such pressure has only increased. Working until 10:00 P.M. and on weekends may have been considered aberrant behavior in 1980, but by 1990 it had become the norm in many organizations. One recently pro-moted middle manager described the pressure as unrelenting. When he assumed the new position, he had an agreement with his boss that he would be available whenever needed and would answer his beeper call within thirty minutes. Little did he know that this was a very literal expectation. He was beeped at all hours, including in the middle of the night, for relatively trivial questions or just to be a sounding board for an idea his boss had. In other words, he needed to be available to assuage his boss's anxiety. When he stopped responding to the beeper in the middle of the night, he began receiving telephone calls. When one call came at 1:30 A.M., his boss apologized, saying that he had simply "lost track of time." In addition, the hours demanded by this job were grueling, leaving very little time for relaxation and family activities. After putting in sixty to eighty hours in a week, the last thing this manager expected or wanted was a telephone call from his boss during the few hours he was at home (and presumably asleep). He decided that the rewards of being promoted were simply not worth the cost, and he requested a downgrade to his previous management level.

There is evidence that top executives do not feel that employees are doing as much as they can. A 1989 survey by Steelcase Inc. found that only 21 percent of top executives felt that employees were doing as much work as they reasonably could, but 49 percent of employees said they were working to their limits. Twenty-five percent of office workers indicated that white-collar jobs have been eliminated, leaving them feeling "pushed to the wall" with work (Hymowitz 1988). All of these pressures resulting from the tough economic times of the late 1980s have made work no longer fun for large proportions of managers, according to a 1991 survey of middle managers and first-line supervisors conducted by *Industry Week* (Work is no fun 1991). Two-thirds of managers said that work was no longer fun, although 60 percent said that work had been fun at one time.

Work/Life Imbalance

All of these demands have caused many employees to experience great difficulty managing their work and their personal lives. With the increase in dual-income families, most families no longer have the luxury of one partner staying at home to take care of young children, supervise school-age children when they return from school, arrange for home repairs, run errands, and make dinner. When both partners work—and work increasingly long hours—home life suffers. A survey conducted for Hilton Hotels Corporation showed the extent to which working people are feeling this crunch. Finding enough time for both work and personal life has become so important that 50 percent of working Americans said that they would be willing to trade a day's pay for an extra day off each week (Hymowitz 1991).

More and more companies have begun to recognize the problems that employees face in balancing work and personal life and have responded by funding various kinds of programs designed to help them cope. Even during the recession of the early 1990s, companies did not cut back on work/family programs and actually increased the amount of resources devoted to working on these issues. However, for the most part the response of employers, even leaders in the work/family arena, has been focused on specific programs. Very few employers have related the problem to the organizational culture that supports workaholism. One employee said that two of her previous employers expected people to "work around the clock, and they couldn't care less if you have a baby or a two-year-old." With regard to family responsibilities, the attitude was "If you're going to bleed, bleed on your own time." Another employee's supervisor was appalled when she became pregnant, telling her that she had planned poorly (Shellenbarger 1991). The problem is that while companies may be addressing work/family issues on a policy and program level, managers in those companies are placing unreasonable demands on subordinates and ignoring their personal lives, as illustrated in the above two examples. The policies and programs that are adopted, progressive as they are, do nothing to change the values and expectations in the culture about long hours. The increasingly stiff competition that companies face is almost an excuse to demand increasingly punishing hours from employees. A poll of CEOs found that they believe that American companies will have to push top managers even harder to keep up with competition. These CEOs also said that managers are working longer hours than they did ten years ago—they have to because of restructuring and increased competition (Solo 1990). If top managers are pushed harder, they will push those under them even harder, and so on down the line. There is an assumption, never questioned, that the only way to respond to competition is to work harder and longer. The alternative—that our obsession with the quantity of time devoted to work may be contributing to our lagging competitiveness—is never considered. The solution is seen as working harder, not working smarter.

WORKAHOLISM AND ADDICTION

Two recent books, *The Addictive Organization* (Schaef and Fassel 1988) and *Working Ourselves to Death: The High Cost of Workaholism and the Rewards of Recovery* (Fassel 1990), explain how workaholism is a true addiction, on both a personal and an organizational level. Workaholics show the same characteristics of addiction that one finds in alcoholics, drug addicts, and compulsive gamblers. Not all addictions are to substances, Schaef and Fassel point out. People can become addicted to processes as well. Examples are compulsive debtors (e.g., gamblers, shoppers), relationship addicts, and workaholics. In all cases, whether the addiction is to a substance or a process, the internal design of the disease is the same.

Denial is one of the hallmarks of addiction. Alcoholics deny the effects of their drinking on their own lives and on their families. Overeaters lie about how much they eat. Workaholics construct elaborate rationalizations for why they must work so much. A workaholic may conveniently "forget" that he stopped by his office while out running a household errand. Like other addicts, workaholics are in denial as well as "dishonest, controlling, judgmental, perfectionistic, self-centered, dualistic in their thinking, confused, crisis oriented, and ultimately spiritually bankrupt" (Schaef and Fassel 1988). All of these characteristics, say the authors, trap a person in the addictive process of the disease.

Workaholics as Managers

When workaholics manage people, they inevitably will abuse subordinates and sometimes peers as well. Machlowitz (1980) describes some of the characteristics of workaholic bosses. For one thing, workaholics tend to be critical and contemptuous of co-workers. The disdain that they communicate is often undeserved and petty. One executive apparently scrutinized and criticized subordinates' attendance records routinely and would comment that they were always calling in sick, that they magnified any little illness in their minds and could not wait to call in sick (Machlowitz 1980). Fassel (1990) relates a similar incident in which workaholics in an organization became furious with their nonworkaholic peers because they worked only forty hours a week and took vacations with their families. The workaholics accused the nonworkaholics of laziness, lack of dedication, and falling down on the job, none of which were true. The attitude of the nonworkaholics (that their jobs were not their entire lives and that it was important for them to have balance) appeared to inflame and infuriate the workaholics, who felt that their approach to work was normal and the correct way to live.

This inability to establish boundaries, which is characteristic of workaholics, is one reason, according to Fassel (1990), that workaholics make poor managers. They do not understand the concept of limits from their own experience. Workaholism runs rampant in their lives, obliterating their own boundaries. Because they can't monitor their own needs, they have no respect for others' needs, especially those of subordinates. Their own experience changes their notion of what is realistic to expect and what is not. They therefore regularly make entirely unrealistic demands and will consistently work people beyond their limits. This process explains Machlowitz's (1980) observations that workaholics demand devotion and dedication to the job even when their subordinates are at home asleep or away on vacation.

The Workaholic Organization

According to Machlowitz (1980), workaholics are intense, energetic, competitive, and driven; have strong self-doubts; prefer labor to leisure; can—and do—work anytime and anywhere; make the most of their time ("the quest to conquer time is constant"); and blur the distinctions between business and pleasure. It is not difficult to see why many companies encourage workaholic tendencies. These are generally the characteristics companies look for in selecting employees with the most potential for advancement. Some might question whether companies would truly want employees who have strong self-doubts, but those doing the selecting judge behavior. They can make assumptions about an employee's level of self-esteem only by inference; what they see is behavior. If self-doubt motivates some employees to work harder (e.g., Brockner, Davy, and Carter 1985), then it is logical that some of those selected on the basis of how hard they are willing to work will have strong self-doubts.

Kanter (1977) discusses the time demands that companies make on their employees as well as the demand that commitment to the company exclude other commitments. Work absorption, Kanter notes, was actively encouraged at the large corporation where she did her research, as well as at many other companies. When she asked employees why they took on extra work, 46 percent indicated that they did so because of the work load itself, and 24 percent because of their commitment to the company. Twenty-one percent indicated that it was their interest in the work content. Kanter notes that it is striking that interest in job content was mentioned least frequently.

Kanter also commented on the effect of this company's policy of frequent geographical transfers on organizational commitment. Transfers reduced the efficacy of commitments other than to the corporation, according to Kanter, and this is one way that companies create loyalty to the firm. Frequent transfers ensured that the corporation provided the only enduring set of social bonds outside of the immediate family.

In fact, this is the major complaint of employees in workaholic organizations, according to Fassel (1990): that the organization has no respect for their private lives. The workaholic organization, according to Fassel, expects to be first in the employee's life and operates consistently with that expectation. Another common complaint of both employees and middle managers is that companies actually foster workaholism. They actively seek and reward workaholic employees.

Many companies are caught in a conflict with regard to their employees' workaholic tendencies. On the one hand, the decision makers may believe intellectually that it is bad for workaholic employees to lead unbalanced lives and therefore may initiate wellness programs, build fitness centers, and send explicit messages that they value employees with balanced lives. On the other hand, when they need something done, they want employees who will get it done no matter what the personal sacrifice. Companies prefer that their employees' commitment to the job comes before all other commitments in their lives. Machlowitz (1980) says that some companies indicate they are beginning to face up to the negative consequences of workaholism; however, their behavior shows that they still encourage workaholic tendencies. Encouraging or even in some cases requiring employees to demonstrate workaholic behavior may be damaging in the long run—not only to the employee's personal life but also to the organization's bottom line.

THE WORKAHOLIC ORGANIZATION AND PRODUCTIVITY

Aside from its effect on people, is overwork due to downsizing resulting in more productive organizations? Hardly. All evidence points in the opposite direction. As Fassel (1990) points out, "It has yet to be proven that the longer a worker toils, the more productive he or she is. The evidence seems to be to the contrary" (p. 107).

Individual Effects

Machlowitz's book *Workaholics: Living With Them, Working With Them* was written to combat the negative stereotype of the workaholic. (In 1980 when this book was published, there was a negative stereotype of workaholics. Whether the stereotype is still a negative one is much less clear in the 1990s.) Even Machlowitz admits that at work, workaholics are often demanding and sometimes not very effective. They tend to exaggerate their own indispensability, which can impede the interests of the organization in the following ways:

- They engage in empire building.
- They fail to hire superbly qualified subordinates who might become rivals.
- They take on too much work and do not delegate duties, even when appropriate.
- They relinquish the duties and privileges of any previous positions only with reluctance, even when they have been promoted.
- They tend not to cooperate or communicate with colleagues.
- At the negative extreme, they may be out only for themselves, unwilling to subordinate their individual goals to the good of the organization as a whole.
- They may be jealous, hostile, resentful, and overly competitive.

It is not difficult to see how these characteristics in a large portion of a company's workforce (or in a few key personnel) could have a negative impact on corporate productivity. As Fassel (1990) points out, research has shown that workaholics do not make a company profitable and in fact end up costing companies money. Some workaholics are erratic in their productivity: they may produce in spurts but have long unproductive periods. Workaholics may look busy because they are moving so fast (indeed, Machlowitz reports that one workaholic said, "I feel I even have to sleep fast"). But this frenetic movement results in mistakes that need to be corrected.

Organizational Effects

With the current emphasis on total quality in companies, the pattern of working fast, making mistakes, and correcting them is referred to as "rework." Although the total quality movement does not specifically refer to workaholism as a cause of this rework phenomenon, it undoubtedly will eventually have to confront workaholism in the workplace, because one of the hallmarks of total quality is finding the root cause of problems, especially problems that result in mistakes, defects, or rework. To the extent that workaholism contributes to these problems, total quality interventions eventually will be forced to reassess the values that lead companies into these unproductive work patterns.

Workaholics also cost companies when they burn out. Fassel (1990) makes the point that whenever corporations promote the workaholic myth for individuals or for the company as a whole, they promote short-term thinking. Such thinking sometimes may produce spectacular short-term gains, but inevitably the long-term effects will be disastrous.

These long-term effects impact not just the individual and the company but also our national productivity. As successive downsizings occurred in the 1980s, and as the survivors began working longer hours, what happened to productivity in the United States? Although the United States still has the highest absolute productivity in the world, its productivity growth rate—the lever of economic development and growth (Prennar 1989)—lags behind its competitors in Europe and Japan.

The gains in manufacturing, although positive, have been disappointingly small. Manufacturing's productivity growth rate in the 1980s was in the range of 3.5 percent to 3.9 percent per year (Prennar 1989; Stewart 1991). A large part of this growth, however, took place in the first few years of the 1980s, slowing to around 3 percent per year by the end of the decade. Productivity rose even more slowly in services—a dismal 0.8 percent per year. Given that people are working 20 percent longer than they did a decade ago, the returns in productivity growth are unacceptably small. Maybe hours spent on the job do not equate to increased productivity after all.

That is, in fact, what all of the research evidence points to. Studies of army officers and oil rig workers indicate that performance drops off after a certain number of hours on the job. The actual number of hours varies, of course, depending on the person and the occupation. However, as one researcher pointed out after interviewing more than one thousand executives in the United States and Britain about their work habits, "Any manager who works over 50 hours a week in my view is turning in less than his best performance" (Worthy 1987).

Companies themselves are also beginning to realize that the strategy of downsizing and increasing workloads for survivors is not bringing them expected gains in productivity and profitability. Cameron found that

two-thirds of downsized organizations studied (in the automobile industry) failed to achieve intended cost reductions and efficiencies (Zemke
1990). The *Wall Street Journal* said it even more strongly: "Layoffs and
corporate downsizing are painful and disruptive to an organization. They
may also be unproductive" (Bennett 1991). A recent survey by Wyatt Co.,
which covered more than one thousand companies and focused on the
five-year period of 1987–91, showed that fewer than half of the companies
that set out to cut costs through restructuring actually did reduce expenses.
Only 32 percent improved profitability, only 22 percent increased productivity, and only 21 percent increased shareholder return on investment
(Bennett 1991).

International Comparisons

The global situation presents even more damning evidence that increased hours do not equal productivity. The top three exporters, West
Germany, the United States and Japan, exhibit very different work patterns. The workaholic Japanese, whom we are presumably emulating,
work an astounding 2,173 hours per year on average. The West Germans
work only 1,668 hours, and Americans are in the middle with 1,890 hours
(Poe and Baker 1990). But the Japanese, who work the hardest, have the
lowest GNP per capita of these top three—$15,030 in U.S. dollars. The
West Germans, who work the least, have the second highest GNP per
capita—$18,370—which approaches the U.S. GNP per capita of $19,800
(Johnson 1991). However, looking at GNP per worker, instead of per
capita, reveals a perfect inverse relationship with hours worked: more time
at work is associated with the lowest GNP per worker. These results are
summarized in Table 1.

Critics of global productivity comparisons that show the United States
near the bottom make several points that they say migitate these findings
(e.g., Warshaw 1984). One is that higher productivity in countries that have
developed recently does not reflect productivity per worker as much as it
reflects new plants, more efficient mechanization, or improved production
technology. Two, high productivity in many European countries (e.g.,
Sweden, West Germany) depends on an infrastructure of imported labor
from the Mediterranean and North African countries ("guest workers"),
whose activities are not factored into the overall productivity. Three, the
rates of alcoholism, suicide, and stress-related diseases in other countries
with a highly organized work society are perhaps even higher than they
are in the United States.

Table 1
Work Patterns and Productivity among the Top Three Exporters

Country	Hours worked (1989)	GNP (1988) $ (Billions)	GNP per capita $	GNP per worker $
W. Germany	1668	1,120	18,370	40,300
U. S.	1890	4,862	19,800	39,900
Japan	2173	1,843	15,030	30,500

Sources: Hours worked from Poe & Baker, 1990

GNP data from Johnson, 1991

Warshaw's first point, that recently industrialized countries may show higher productivity due to new plants and so forth is valid. It will be addressed directly in the next section, which examines the Japanese work ethic and demonstrates that the perception of superior Japanese productivity does not hold up under closer inspection. The second point, that some countries' seemingly higher productivity may depend on an unseen infrastructure of unofficial imported labor, is not as valid as it first may appear because the United States also has a large, undocumented, "shadow" workforce whose activities are not counted in the official calculations of productivity. This workforce is composed of illegal aliens, upon whom our agricultural sector—where American productivity predominantly resides—so greatly depends. In fact, this undocumented workforce is so large and so necessary to production that it has been speculated that large portions of American agriculture would grind to a halt without it. Therefore American productivity also is dependent on a large infrastructure of unofficial, imported labor, largely from Mexico.

The third point made by Warshaw, that alcoholism, suicide, and stress-related diseases are even more frequent in other industrialized countries whose productivity may appear higher than our own, is also a good one. Such phenomena may not be included in how a nation's productivity is measured, but they are part of the price that is paid for work policies and practices. The impact may be felt most of the time on an individual level, but perhaps only up to a certain point. When individual pathologies are so frequent as to demonstrate a pattern on a national level, one is forced to wonder what the collective impact is on a country's productivity. Perhaps a new definition of productivity must be conceptualized, one that takes into account the collective individual costs of the national work pattern.

Working Themselves to Death

A more sinister by-product of the workaholic pattern has come to light in Japan. The phenomenon known as *karoshi*, or death from overwork, has begun to gain media attention in Japan as well as in this country. Although only recently catapulted into the national consciousness through publicity, the phenomenon has been known among Japanese middle managers for an undetermined length of time. *Karoshi* victims' families have made compensation claims against the government and employers. In 1988, the government awarded compensation in twenty-nine cases of death or disability that resulted from something other than industrial accidents (Sanger 1990). This figure is so low that many critics claim that it proves the government is covering up the extent of the problem. Lawyers and doctors organized a campaign for government action—the National Defense Counsel for Victims of Karoshi—and set up a *karoshi* hot line in 1988. This hot line received more than three hundred calls on its first day of operation. One of the founders of this group is Chikanobu Okamura, a lawyer. He encountered his first *karoshi* labor compensation case in 1979. In this case, a bread baker working the night shift died from a heart attack, and the court ruled that the three consecutive years that he had spent on the night shift had fatally aggravated his hardening arteries, entitling his family to labor compensation. This case, says Okamura, told him that *karoshi* was to become an important social issue (Makihara 1991).

What is this oppressive work pattern buying the Japanese? The progress they have made since the end of World War II in becoming a global economic power is astonishing indeed. However, their gains may cause them to appear superior to the rest of the world only because they started out so far behind the rest of the industrialized world economically. When the productivity numbers are examined more closely, as above, we see that their perceived superiority in productivity is illusory. In fact, now that Japan has become one of the top global players and has achieved some measure of parity with the West, there are increasing reports that the Japanese are beginning to suffer some of the same quality and productivity problems as the rest of the industrialized nations.

Here is the harsh reality: the average Japanese worker puts in five hundred more hours at work over the course of a year than does the average German worker. Not only does this not yield higher productivity for the country as a whole, but it may literally be killing the worker. According to Japan's Ministry of Health and Welfare, *karoshi* may be responsible for 10 percent of all deaths of employed men in Japan, making it the second-largest killer of that population (Fassel 1990, quoting the *Chicago Tribune*). It would be hard to imagine a more dramatic kind of employee abuse.

SUMMARY

The workaholic culture supported by many organizations in the United States is damaging the productivity of individuals, organizations, and the nation as a whole. When faced with tougher competitive pressures, it is easy to buy into the seductive notion that working harder (i.e., working longer) will result in greater productivity. It is certainly far easier to embrace that notion than it is to figure out how to work smarter. The denial process that is such a basic aspect of addictions, including work addiction, prevents us from seeing the futility of such a strategy. But if we are to become truly competitive, we must learn how to work smarter, not just harder.

The distorted thinking that causes managers to demand longer hours from employees is responsible for a huge amount of employee abuse. Managers are under increasing pressure to produce more with less (i.e., fewer employees). Frequently, they simply turn around and translate this pressure on them into a very literal demand on subordinates to work more hours. Not only does this wreak havoc on the personal lives and health of overworked employees, but it has a negative impact on the organization as well.

It is incumbent on human resource managers not only to raise the level of awareness within companies of the destructive effects of a workaholic culture but also to provide the tools with which to build more positive strategies to respond to competition. Fortunately, some of the same approaches that offer the potential to address the root causes of quality and productivity problems are the same ones that can eradicate employee abuse. An integrated emphasis on total quality, for instance, can change the corporate culture while improving business processes, thereby supporting the value of working smarter. Employee involvement is a major part of a total quality effort. If employees see that while they are contributing to finding solutions to business problems, management is also working at eliminating organizational and systemic barriers to quality, employee commitment can increase and peak performance can result. And isn't peak performance what management is truly after anyway?

REFERENCES

Ansberry, C. 1989. Risky business: Workplace injuries proliferate as concerns push people to produce. *Wall Street Journal* (June 16): A1.

Bennett, A. 1988. Is your job making you sick? *Wall Street Journal* (April 22): 1R.

———. 1991. Downsizing doesn't necessarily bring an upswing in corporate profitability. *Wall Street Journal* (June 6): B1.

Brockner, J.; Davy, J.; and Carter, C. 1985. Layoff, self-esteem and survivor guilt: Motivational, affective and attitudinal consequences. *Organizational Behavior and Human Decision Processes* 36: 229–44.

Fassel, D. 1990. *Working ourselves to death: The high cost of workaholism and the rewards of recovery.* San Francisco: Harper & Row.

Hymowitz, C. 1988. Executives out of touch with office workers? *Wall Street Journal* (June 16): B1.

———. 1991. Trading fat paychecks for free time. *Wall Street Journal* (August 5): B1.

Job engorgement: Job redesign for the '90's. 1991. *Decisions . . . Decisions* (a newsletter published by Management Decision Systems) (Spring): 2.

Johnson, O., ed. 1991. *Information please almanac.* Boston: Houghton Mifflin.

Kanter, R. M. 1977. *Men and women of the corporation.* New York: Basic Books.

Kilborn, P. T. 1990. The work week grows: Tales from the digital treadmill. *New York Times* (June 3): 1E.

Machlowitz, M. 1980. *Workaholics: Living with them, working with them.* Reading, Mass.: Addison-Wesley.

Makihara, K. 1991. Death of a salaryman. *InHealth* (May-June): 41–50.

Poe, R. and Baker, E. L. 1990. Fast forward. *Across the Board* (October): 3–4.

Prennar, K. 1989. The productivity paradox. *Business Week* (June 6): 100–2.

Sanger, D. E. 1990. Tokyo tries to find out if "salarymen" are working themselves to death. *New York Times* (March 19): A8.

Schaef, A. W. and Fassel, D. 1988. *The addictive organization.* San Francisco: Harper & Row.

Shellenbarger, S. 1991. More job seekers put family needs first. *Wall Street Journal* (November 15): B1.

Solo, S. 1990. Stop whining and get back to work. *Fortune* (March 12): 49–50.

Stewart, T. A. 1991. The new American century: Where we stand. *Fortune* (Special Issue Spring-Summer): 12–23.

Warshaw, L. J. 1984. Managing stress. In *Stress and Productivity*, edited by Krinsky et al., 15–54. New York: Human Sciences Press.

Work is no fun. 1991. *Personnel Journal* (May): 17.

Worthy, F. S. 1987. You're probably working too hard. *Fortune* (April 27): 133–40.

Zemke, R. 1990. The ups and downs of downsizing. *Training* (November): 27–34.

7

Policies, Procedures, and Management Practices

Organizations do not set out to be abusive to their workforces. However, in the course of pursuing legitimate business goals, such as reducing costs, increasing flexibility, and eliminating workplace injuries, they sometimes do things that result in abusive impact on employees. This often happens when people, in trying to achieve a goal, become so task-focused as to ignore the impact of how they accomplish it. That helps in achieving the goal in the short term but occasionally has a negative effect on a working relationship. The same thing can happen on an institutional level when a company focuses on achieving a specific goal. This chapter will concentrate on the negative impact on employees of certain policies, procedures, and practices that are adopted for very good reasons but may end up doing more harm than good.

MANAGED MEDICAL CARE

In an attempt to control costs, many companies have instituted controls in their medical plans. Many of these plans use preferred provider networks, in which physician membership is limited. There have been instances in which a physician wanted to join a network in order to continue treating patients working for companies whose plans were switching to that network. Sometimes these physicians were not allowed to join because the network was "full" in that geographical area, and their patients were forced by the plan to find a new doctor. Employees who have been seeing a particular doctor for years have had to switch because of a new health plan their company adopted. Such plans discourage personal choice, which is very important in the doctor-patient relationship.

Many of the effects of managed medical care plans are merely annoying, but others raise the possibility of substandard care. One employee whose company switched to Plan A, a managed care plan, had to choose a new doctor on the list of Plan A providers. The employee was told by this doctor's office that she could see her doctor only on Wednesday mornings, because that was the only time he was in the office. The employee was aware that this particular doctor and his partner had two other offices in different locations and did not expect that he would spend all of his time in the one office where she saw him, but she found it difficult to believe that he really would only be in that office one half-day per week. Such infrequent office hours would not justify the costs of maintaining an office in that upscale community. She suspected that he was actually seeing patients there more frequently but had chosen to limit the amount of time that he would be available to Plan A patients. That was a reasonable assumption, because of the following features of Plan A.

The plan limited the amount that doctors were reimbursed for their services to what it called "reasonable and customary fees." The amounts that the plan would pay were usually lower than the amounts generally charged by doctors in that area. Also, the patients in Plan A were responsible for a small "copayment" each time they visited the doctor, but they paid no more—the plan covered the rest. Physicians had to agree to this arrangement in order to belong to the network of preferred providers. In other words, the physician most likely would not be paid the full amount for his or her services by Plan A. If the insurance company did not pay the entire amount charged, the physician could not expect the patient to be responsible for the rest. Given these features, a doctor would earn less by treating a patient covered by Plan A than he or she might by treating a patient with a different kind of insurance coverage. Doctors, like anyone else, are motivated to maximize their income, and they face substantial opportunity costs each time they treat a patient covered by a plan that pays less than they usually charge. It stands to reason that a doctor who already has a busy practice and agrees to join such a network of preferred providers, would limit the amount of time he or she is willing to spend treating patients on whom he or she loses money.

Certain policies of managed care plans create difficult situations and major inconveniences for employees. One way in which these plans try to keep costs down is by inserting an approval step in the process of receiving care. Some plans do this by requiring that all care be coordinated by a primary care physician who, each time care is needed, decides whether to treat a specific condition or send the patient to a specialist. If the employee skips the primary care physician and goes directly to any other doctor, the plan will penalize the employee with a lower level of reimbursement. This often results in two office visits for the employee rather than one (the first to the primary care physician, the second to the specialist). In some cases, this would happen anyway, regardless of the plan, because the employee may not know what is wrong or what kind of specialist is needed. In other cases it is not necessary at all. For instance, an employee with a recurrent dermatological condition may have an ongoing relationship with a dermatologist. When symptoms recur, the employee knows that he needs to see the dermatologist. However, because of the managed care plan, he is forced to see his primary care physician first, in order to obtain the approval to see the dermatologist. This extra step wastes the employee's time and results in delayed care. In some cases, that could make a difference in the long-term prognosis.

Other plans require preapproval for certain procedures (i.e., the doctor must consult a plan administrator for permission to proceed). Both the doctor and the patient can eventually adjust to this procedure, and the doctor need not feel that her competency is being questioned any more than she would if the patient asked for a second opinion. However, there has to be an impact on the doctor-patient relationship when the insurance company requires a halt in the treatment plan until it can be approved by an administrator who has less medical training than the physician, and who knows neither doctor nor patient.

The review procedure in many plans can have more damaging effects than mere embarrassment for the employee. Critics say that these restrictions interfere with care providers' medical decisions because reviewers and insurers sometimes put cost considerations ahead of patient needs ("Managed Care" 1991; Freudenheim 1991). A recent lawsuit in California involved a patient who died from complications of chronic drug abuse after being released prematurely from a hospital's drug abuse program. A medical review company had told the patient's doctor that more time in the hospital was "not justified or approved," and the insurance company therefore would not pay any more benefits. The appeals court found that the review company's decision was a substantial factor in the patient's death, and that a cost-limitation program was "permitted to corrupt medical judgment" (Freudenheim 1991). When the review process results in decisions that appear to put employees' health at risk, employees increasingly will perceive managed care as discount medicine. They will tend to believe that their employers' cost concerns are the basis for critical decisions, and this may result in increased lawsuits against both employers and insurers ("Conference Advises HR" 1990).

Another area of medical care affected by cost considerations is the use of generic drugs. Many insurance plans require the use of generic drugs when available in an effort to reduce costs. This can create problems for some patients, and claims for damages from the use of generic drugs are increasing (Fine 1990). Generic drugs are not always exactly like their name-brand counterparts. In certain generic drugs, the standards and tolerances are somewhat different. Sometimes they use different preservatives, which can result in unforeseen allergic reactions. For some patients and some medical conditions, a doctor may choose to use only a name-brand drug, but many insurers refuse to pay for anything other than the generic. If the medical plan imposes such restrictions on physicians, liability for any resulting injury may fall on the insurer as well as on the doctor—and sometimes on the employer. There are also some drugs for which there is no generic, and some managed care plans still refuse to pay for them. This is a case of slavish devotion to bureaucratic rules and an absence of common sense. The end result is an unfair situation for the employee.

Another example of managed care requirements creating inconveniences for employees is that the preferred provider network includes not only physicians but hospitals and laboratories as well. One employee found that under her company's new plan, she could no longer have tests done at a lab that was conveniently located near her home. Instead, the closest lab that was a member of the network was an hour away.

Some plans have features that can result in questionable treatment decisions. An employee, who had recently switched physicians to accommodate his company's new medical plan, became ill with flulike symptoms. When after five days his symptoms began to get worse, he called his new doctor, who told him to wait it out. Since this was a Friday, he was quite concerned about what he should do if he became significantly worse over the weekend. During the course of that day, he became progressively sicker. His doctor was still telling him not to go to the hospital. He finally insisted, got permission to go to the emergency room, and was admitted. The diagnosis was septicemia. The infection had first spread to his bladder and then entered his bloodstream. Had he listened to his doctor and waited through the weekend, he probably would have died. While in the hospital he was informed by more than one practitioner that with his medical plan, physicians get paid for keeping people out of the hospital. Should a patient become ill enough to require hospitalization, deductions are made to the doctor's fee. That is one way that the medical plan, and therefore the employer, saves money by "managing" care. This method of cost savings potentially endangers the health of employees.

No one would argue that there should be no accountability in the medical profession, but the ways companies choose to force more accountability are abusive to both doctors and to employees. They are interfering in the doctor-patient relationship in negative ways, which potentially can result in substandard medical care. Furthermore, when the causes of the astronomical increases in medical costs are examined more carefully, one sees that a large portion of the increased costs are due to stress-related illnesses (see Chapter 10). Companies themselves are responsible for a good portion of this increase due to the pressures they have been imposing on managers and employees in order to achieve short-term goals. While increased competition has changed the environment in many companies, there are better ways to respond to the new competitive threats. American companies have chosen a strategy of short-term thinking and solutions rather than a long-term approach based on investments in quality processes and human capital. These choices have led American companies to downsize to the point where quality and innovation cannot flourish, people are too rushed to provide maximum productivity, and the resulting pressure-cooker environment gives rise to abusive management practices. Then when medical costs increase, as they inevitably must when unrealistic demands continually are made on people, employees are further abused by restrictive managed medical care plans that put cost considerations ahead of health.

CONTINGENT WORKFORCE

The last decade has seen an enormous increase in the number of workers without full-time ties to employers. These workers include temporary and part-time workers, contractors, and anyone working under a no-strings-attached arrangement. These workers have been dubbed the "contingent workforce." Companies have increasingly turned to this workforce because it is "expandable and expendable" (Russakoff and Skrzycki 1988). Contingent workers grew by about 14 percent in the 1980s to thirty million, or about one-fourth of the U.S. workforce (Rose 1991). These workers also usually have no benefits or reduced benefits, providing further cost savings to employers. Over the last twenty years, there has been a 121 percent increase in the number of workers who have no fixed schedule and no medical benefits (Mandel 1991).

Not surprisingly, many workers in the contingent workforce find themselves there involuntarily. They may be unable to find full-time work and so they make do with whatever employment arrangement they can find. Most of the growth in part-time employment since 1970 is accounted for by involuntary part-time workers (Tilly 1991).

Tilly makes a distinction between short-time, retention, and secondary part-time jobs. *Short-time* part-time work, frequently referred to as *work sharing* among those who support flexible work options, is used during a business downturn, when employers temporarily reduce workers' hours. This is done as an alternative to layoffs. When business picks up again, full-time hours are restored. This type of work makes up a very small fraction of part-time employment—less than one-tenth.

Retention part-time jobs are generally good jobs created to attract and retain valued employees who, for one reason or another, are unable to work full-time. These jobs are characterized by high compensation, high productivity, and low turnover, and tend to be offered only to highly skilled workers. The typical situation is a woman with young children at home who has worked full-time in the past and anticipates working full-time again after the children are older. This type of part-time employment also comprises a small portion of part-time employment.

The most prevalent type of part-time employment is secondary part-time employment, which is characterized by low skill requirements, low pay and benefits, low productivity, and high turnover. This is the typical low-level service sector job with little opportunity for advancement. Low compensation and scheduling flexibility are why employers use this form of part-time employment. This is also where most of the involuntary part-timers will be found. These jobs are the dead-end, stop-gap jobs from which people escape as soon as they are able to find something better.

Using a contingent workforce to supplement a company's full-time workforce has enabled greater flexibility and an enhanced ability to provide security to the company's full-time workers. But reasons for the growth of the contingent workforce go even deeper than that. The contingent workforce is part of a major restructuring of work and the shift from manufacturing into services. Tilly (1991) asserts that the primary reason companies use a contingent workforce is to cut labor costs and enhance staffing flexibility, not to maintain a stable labor force, at least in some areas of work. Additional reasons are that scheduling difficulties can be solved most effectively by using short-hour employees, and that such a workforce can be used as a union-busting device. Levitan and Conway (1988) believe that some employers, under the pretext of flexibility, may be using contingent workers to undermine unions, pay levels, or fringe benefits among full-time employees.

Tilly (1991) reports that in 1989, part-time employees comprised almost one-fifth of the U.S. workforce. This equates to about twenty million people working in the nonagricultural sectors of the economy, or 18.1 percent of all workers. Furthermore, almost five million were involuntary part-time workers who would have preferred a full-time job. The effects of involuntary part-time work can be financially devastating to an individual and to families. Consider the following statistics:

- One in five part-time workers heads a family (Levitan and Conway 1988).

- More than one-third of involuntary part-time workers have no health insurance. In many cases when insurance is provided, it excludes workers' families (Rose 1991).

- Eight in ten part-time workers are not covered by their employers' pension plan (Levitan and Conway 1988).

- Part-time jobs tend to be lower-paid jobs. Part-timers earn about 58 percent as much per hour as full-timers (Tilly 1991). This puts many of them at the poverty level. In 1988, 40 percent of single-parent families headed by part-timers had incomes below the poverty level, and 26 percent received public aid (Rose 1991). Part-time workers comprise more than half of those working for minimum and subminimum wages (Levitan and Conway 1988).

The contingent workforce is expanding not only in numbers, but also in the types of jobs and skills that it taps. In recent years, a new development has taken hold and grown: contingent managers and professionals. *Business Week* has declared that the corporate career, once a solid foundation for middle-class families, is in shambles, and advises those affected to transform themselves into "itinerant professionals who sell their human capital on the open market" (Nussbaum 1991). People who find themselves in this situation are responsible not just for earning money from their professional services, but also for their own health benefits and retirement funding.

These trends raise some disturbing and complex issues. The effect of a growing contingent workforce could be a polarization of workers and of society into two groups: a highly paid, highly skilled portion, and a low-paid, low-skilled underclass of workers with few options, minimal leverage in the marketplace, and decreasing earning power (Russakoff and Skrzycki 1988).

Companies say that they need the flexibility that a contingent workforce provides. They have responded to competitive threats by cutting costs, which in corporate America usually means getting rid of people. In order to do the work, they supplement the remaining full-time workforce with a flexible contingent workforce. In the short run they may see increased profits, but what about the long-term view? There are tremendous and possibly unquantifiable social costs in having a large contingent workforce that constitutes an economic underclass. In the long run, supporting this underclass will drain more and more of society's resources, leaving fewer resources available for investment in new business opportunities and shrinking potential domestic markets for high-tech, sophisticated products and services. A low-paid underclass of contingent workers with decreasing earning power also has decreasing buying power. A circular process could evolve: economic competition drives cost-cutting measures, which moves more people into the underclass, which limits their buying power, which shrinks demand for products and services, which lowers business profits, which drives further cost-cutting, and so on. In the end, the process makes American society as a whole less competitive and lowers the national standard of living.

There are no easy answers to these problems. As Kathleen Christensen, a nationally known expert on the contingent workforce, points out, it's not as simple as the "big, bad employer and the victim worker" (Russakoff and Skrzycki 1988). There is a fundamental restructuring of work and the workforce occurring that is driven by a shift into a service economy. However, that there are larger economic and social forces operating here does not relieve business of responsibility. Our society is becoming more global and more interdependent very rapidly. What companies do affects not just their own competitiveness but the competitiveness of American society and of individuals, who are not just employees but also customers. *Business Week* also points out that our rivals in the global marketplace, the Japanese and the Europeans, are also striving for increased productivity, but not at the expense of their human capital ("When the Bonds" 1991). Japanese and European companies manage to retain lifelong loyalty and commitment among their employees—and still beat their American competitors. Clearly, the workforce slashing strategy is not necessary to succeed in the global marketplace. There are choices available, and American business needs to find ways to increase competitiveness and raise the standard of living, not lower it.

SAFETY

The competitive pressures that are driving cost-cutting and downsizing are also increasing the focus on productivity and speed. Many safety experts are concerned, having noticed some alarming increases in injury rates. They attribute this rise to business's response to competition. Some of the business conditions that they see contributing to rising injury rates are smaller work crews, more overtime, faster assembly lines, and the unrelenting drive to produce (Ansberry 1989). Some of the most dramatic examples of the consequences of this drive for speedier production come from the steel industry, where employees have been killed in grisly and avoidable accidents. In several cases workers were killed by stacks of steel that fell on them. The steel was stacked too high because the company was running out of storage room, and the supervisors did not respond when told of the situation. As one employee testified, "It was production first and then we worried about safety" (Ansberry 1991).

A meat-packing plant was fined by the Occupational Safety and Health Administration (OSHA) for "willfully ignoring" cumulative trauma disorders that workers developed from the repetitive motion on its high-speed assembly lines, and for not giving injured workers enough time to recover. Assembly-line speed had increased as much as 84 percent in some areas of the plant without a significant increase in staff, and during that period plantwide injuries increased 51 percent (Ansberry 1989).

Companies' labor strategies may also contribute to the rise in injuries. Trimming the workforce often results in increasing demands on those who are left, including more overtime. In the steel industry, overtime has become the norm. Steelmakers are reluctant to add new jobs even as demand increases for fear of losing productivity gains. A study on causes of injuries found that more overtime and employee turnover were implicated in 93 percent of the injuries examined (Ansberry 1989).

Some workers claim that other contributors to accidents are employers' removal of the safety mechanisms that hinder faster output. One worker lost four fingers when his hand was caught in a machine from which safety guards and a clutch regulating speed had been removed (Ansberry 1989). In another case, a devastating fire in a chicken-processing plant in North Carolina killed twenty-five people. A state investigator found that locked doors aggravated the death toll. One of the doors was locked by dead bolts in two places on the outside. This plant also did not have an automatic sprinkler system, properly marked fire exits, or a fire evacuation plan (Taylor 1991b). It was not clear why exit doors were locked in a factory in which oil heated to 400 degrees in deepfat fryers poses a significant fire risk. Employees claimed that managers kept doors locked in order to prevent the low-wage employees from stealing chicken parts (Taylor 1991a).

Office jobs are not immune from safety considerations. Repetitive motion injuries, especially from workers who use computer keyboards, have been increasing. The U.S. Bureau of Labor Statistics reported eighty-seven thousand cases in 1990—triple the number from five years before (Kirp 1990). Those numbers may be an alarming underestimate of the true number of such injuries. A survey of doctors in Santa Clara County found seven thousand cases of carpal tunnel syndrome, one form of repetitive motion disorder, but only seventy-two of those cases, or 1 percent, had been included in the labor statistics (Kirp 1990). Some observers claim that business at first tried to deny or ignore the issue of keyboard-induced trauma entirely and then fought requirements to protect workers from the conditions that induce the injuries (Kirp 1990; Mandel 1991a, 1991b). It has now been recognized as a significant health threat, and OSHA is beginning to develop regulations to cover a wide range of ergonomics issues at the workplace ("Capital Wrapup" 1991c).

Given these threats to safety in the workplace, it is ironic indeed that many employers are using accident records to screen applicants in an attempt to limit medical and workers' compensation costs (Moore 1991). This practice is growing nationwide. The rationale behind it is to screen out workers who are unfit or at high risk for accidents, as well as those who are likely to abuse the system with fraudulent claims that are difficult to confirm, such as stress or back strain (Fuchsberg 1990). Critics say, however, that it can result in companies unfairly and illegally discriminating against applicants who have made legitimate claims.

This practice works as follows: Private firms create databases on injury records from workers' compensation and injury-related lawsuits. Employers pay for background checks on prospective employees in order to see if they have a history of on-the-job injuries. At least one consumer group is targeting the firms that offer information from these databases, charging that the files constitute a blacklist, and that workers who desire to return to the workforce are being rejected even though they are healthy.

It is conceivable that the following scenario could happen: An employer pressures workers to produce faster, and managers ignore safety concerns in order to keep up production. A worker is seriously injured as a result. Unable to return to his previous job, the workers' compensation system retrains him in a new line of work. But when he is ready to seek employment in his new skill area, he is rejected time and again by employers who make injury background checks and find that he filed a claim under workers' compensation.

There surely are workers who move from job to job, claiming injuries and collecting money each time. It is reasonable to expect that employers will want to avoid hiring such workers if they can, but no one knows what percentage of all injury claims are truly fraudulent. If it is a very small portion, then this practice is wasteful as well as unjust. There are probably far better ways of identifying the real malingerers without stigmatizing everyone who has ever been injured at work. Once again, this is a case in which the obvious strategy of rejecting workers likely to file claims is short-sighted and does not address the root causes of injuries in the workplace. Rather than putting resources into checking backgrounds of all applicants in order to identify the true bad apples, companies would be far better off putting that effort into creating a safer workplace and reducing their liability by implementing mechanisms and incentives for working safely.

Several companies have actually done this and reduced their injury rates significantly. By combining a total quality approach with simple behavioral techniques (providing positive consequences for safe behavior rather than negative consequences for unsafe behavior), they have reduced accident and injury rates significantly. A Monsanto plant scrapped its traditional safety program, realizing that it was not working, and put its energy into discovering the root causes of common injuries. It established a peer reward system to reinforce safe behavior and injuries dropped by 76 percent in three years (Milbank 1991). A manufacturing company achieved similar results by throwing out its punishment-oriented safety program and setting safety goals, followed by holding celebrations when the goals were met (Hatcher 1991). Education and employee involvement were cornerstones of its renewed commitment to safety, with employees contributing suggestions to make their workplace safer. Discussions were held with employees who had had more than one accident in the past year, but the emphasis was on explaining and getting a commitment rather than on threatening or cajoling. In three years it cut its accident rate by 77 percent and reduced workers' compensation costs by 69 percent.

These solutions may sound overly simplistic to some, but they work. Traditional safety programs at most companies fit right into the aversive behavior control model discussed in Chapter 4. This society is so oriented toward punishment for incorrect behavior that it is sometimes difficult to believe the enormous behavior changes that can be effected by simply changing to a strategy of positive behavior control—one that includes constant feedback and positive reinforcement. The practice of screening accident records is merely another example of our cultural bias to punish unwanted behavior rather than rewarding desired behavior. Not only does this strategy not solve the problem, it probably does not lower injury rates or workers' compensation costs, much less build employee commitment to a safe workplace. But here is some hard evidence that it is possible to do it all—not by screening out "bad employees" but by instituting some very simple behavioral principles. Not only did workers reduce costs at these plants, they also developed a sense of pride and commitment rather than the suspiciousness and resentment that is usually felt where punishing management practices occur.

SUMMARY

This chapter has documented many instances of actions taken by organizations that result in negative impacts on employees. In some cases, the negative impact extends beyond the employee body to society at large. An example of this wider impact is the increasing reliance on a contingent workforce, which affects America's competitiveness and standard of living. In the future, analyses of cost/benefit need to be done in a much larger systemic context, focusing on far more than immediate, short-term cost savings. Human resource managers can be instrumental in focusing their employers' attention to some of the long-term, insidious effects of organizational decisions not only on costs but on productivity and competitiveness.

REFERENCES

Ansberry, C. 1989. Risky business: Workplace injuries proliferate as concerns push people to produce. *Wall Street Journal* (June 16): A1.

————. 1991. Hazardous duty: Nucor Steel's sheen is marred by deaths of workers at plants. *Wall Street Journal* (May 10): A1.

Baker, B. 1991. U.S. jobless figures fail to add "hidden unemployed." *Los Angeles Times* (April 11): A1.

Capital wrapup: Job safety. 1991c. *Business Week* (July 29): 41.

Conference advises HR on health care issues. 1990. *Human Resource Management News* (June 23): 2.

Fine, B. 1990. Generic drugs: Money-saving answer or liability risk? *The Halsted Harbinger* (Summer 1990): 5.

Freudenheim, M. 1991. Doctors press states to curb reviews of procedures' costs. *New York Times* (February 13): C1.

Fuchsberg, G. 1990. Employers' use of accident records raises specter of black-listed workers. *Wall Street Journal* (July 16): B1.

Hatcher, E. 1991. Positive safety. *Training* (July): 39–41.

Kirp, D. L. 1990. VDTs: Short-handled hoes for white collars. *San Francisco Examiner* (December 23): A19.

Levitan, S. A. and Conway, E. A. 1988. Part-timers: Living on half-rations. *Challenge* (May-June): 9–16.

Managed care: Successes and criticism. 1991. *Human Resource Management News* (September 2): 2.

Mandel, B. 1991a. Big business, women's feet and health care. *San Francisco Examiner* (March 10): B3.

————. 1991b. What books don't tell us about bosses. *San Francisco Examiner* (June 23): B2.

Milbank, D. 1991. Companies turn to peer pressure to cut injuries as psychologists join the battle. *Wall Street Journal* (March 29): B1.

Moore, M. J. 1991. Accident records as a screening device: The search for "safe" employees. *Human Resources Professional* (Spring): 13–15.

Nussbaum, B. 1991. I'm worried about my job! A career survival kit. *Business Week* (October 7): 94–104.

Rose, J. 1991. More part-time, but not by choice. *Los Angeles Times* (September): S12.

Russakoff, D. and Skrzycki, C. 1988. Growing pains in the "contingent work force." *Washington Post* (February 11): A1.

Taylor, P. 1991a. Ashes and accusations: Charges fly over factory fire deaths. *Washington Post* (September 5): A1.

————. 1991b. City officials urge criminal probe of safety lapses at fatal fire scene. *Washington Post* (September 7): A3.

Tilly, C. 1991. Reasons for the continuing growth of part-time employment. *Monthly Labor Review* (March): 10–18.

When the bonds of loyalty are broken (Editorial). *Business Week* (October 7): 158.

8

Potential for New Forms of Abuse: Employee Testing

Businesses have become very interested in various kinds of tests administered in the workplace to gain information about employees. Ability testing is not new in companies, especially larger ones. Applicants are often screened with aptitude and ability tests before the company makes an investment in continuing with the employment process. Workplace testing has provided many benefits for both employers and employees. Basic skills testing has enabled employers to screen applicants most likely to succeed at various jobs and has led to literacy-training programs for current employees. Certain psychological or behavior tests have been used for development purposes or in team-building efforts.

One driving force behind business's interest in screening tests has been the increase in negligent hiring actions in recent years (Gold and Unger 1991; Zemke 1990). Negligent hiring cases are those in which an employer is held liable for an employee's harmful behavior toward a customer or fellow employee on the grounds that the company could have taken steps to avoid hiring a person who would be likely to do such harm. This situation has prompted companies to be very concerned about gaining information about prospective candidates.

However, all tests have their limits. As contemporary social trends have increased concern about employees' behavior both on and off the job, companies have turned to testing as a way to weed out undesirables. This chapter will illustrate several ways in which an overly strong reliance on testing without a correspondingly robust understanding of their limitations can lead to employee abuse.

DRUG TESTING

The use of illegal drugs is a legitimate social and corporate concern. The National Institute on Drug Abuse has estimated that alcohol and drug abuse costs the United States more than $100 billion annually (Pace and Smits 1989). Notwithstanding the enormous social and economic costs of tolerating a large population of addicts, there are real safety concerns when an employee's impaired performance on the job can affect others, such as in public transportation, in a power plant, and so forth.

Corporations have reason to be concerned about substance abuse among their employees. In fact, there is a long-standing history of corporate concern over alcohol abuse, which led to the development of employee assistance programs. However, it is only with the more recent emphasis on illegal drugs that companies have become concerned enough to initiate drug testing, either among applicants for employment or among current employees.

Statistics on the frequency of drug testing vary, particularly since companies test different populations and use differing methodologies of testing. Some test applicants only, some test applicants and employees. Among those testing employees, some test randomly, others test only "for cause." Surveys have shown that over half of all companies have drug testing programs. The 1991 American Management Association (AMA) Survey on Workplace Testing revealed that 63 percent of firms perform drug tests on employees—up from 52 percent in 1989 ("More Firms Testing" 1991; Greenberg 1990), and the Conference Board reported in May 1990 that 55 percent of major U.S. companies actively test "new applicants and employees" or are about to do so (Poe and Baker 1990). The *Wall Street Journal* reports that 96 percent of the nation's top one hundred companies screen applicants (Feinstein 1990; Conte 1991).

How this testing is accomplished may be more important than the fact that a program exists. Evidence for the prevalence of types of tests done (i.e., urinalysis, blood analysis, performance testing, hair analysis, pupillary reaction tests, etc.) is primarily anecdotal at this point, although it appears that most firms rely on urinalysis. In the following discussion, drug testing refers to urinalysis or other such methods that use body products, including body fluids. Alternative testing procedures that are performance-sensitive will be discussed later in this chapter.

Issues in Drug Testing

There are a variety of issues involved in drug testing employees. The following sections will discuss each in turn.

Random Testing versus Testing for Cause. The case for random testing (i.e., surprise tests on a randomly selected sample of employees) is strongest for industries or services involving public safety. The previously cited AMA study reports that, of those firms that test current employees, 20 percent do so randomly, up from 10 percent one year previously ("More Firms Testing" 1991). However, at least three disadvantages to random testing have been identified: it creates resentment among employees; it is not likely to yield many offenders; and it can be an invasion of privacy (Kupfer 1988).

The disadvantages of random testing probably outweigh the benefits for firms without direct responsibility for public safety. Management in these companies would be well advised to eliminate random testing in favor of testing only for probable cause, and then only if the companies have a rehabilitative approach rather than an identify-and-punish approach.

Accuracy of Tests. Problems in the accuracy of current drug-testing procedures have been cited widely (Kupfer 1988; Maltby 1990; Zetlin 1991). The Centers for Disease Control report widespread problems in accuracy for urinalysis in particular (Maltby 1990). These problems in accuracy result in false positives (indicating drugs in a person's system when in reality there are none) and false negatives (indicating no drugs in a person's system when in reality there are). Up to 10 percent of all samples tested are false positives (Kupfer 1988), which could bring negative consequences to innocent employees, unless the company has a policy of validating positive findings—that is, returning them to the lab for more accurate confirmatory tests. Unfortunately, many companies do not validate positive findings—estimates of the percentage of companies that do not retest range between 10 percent (Greenberg 1990) and 33 percent (Kupfer 1988). A false positive that is not corrected with further testing could result in someone not being hired or being fired, disciplined, or labeled as a drug abuser when in reality he or she does not use drugs at all.

Tests' Inability to Distingish Illegal Drugs from Certain Prescribed Substances. Related to the above cited accuracy problems is another problem: screening tests are very sensitive, they are not very specific (Kupfer 1988). The tests screen for by-products of illegal drugs that show up in blood and urine. The presence of a by-product does not necessarily mean that the person has ingested an illegal drug. Many legal substances, including some prescription drugs, can yield a positive result. Some companies ask the person being tested to list any current medications they are using. However, this is not an ideal corrective strategy. Since by-products of certain legal drugs stay in the system for long periods of time, someone may forget that he or she had codeine two weeks previously after a root canal procedure. Or what about a person who is on a psychoactive drug because of a mood disorder, or is unmarried and on birth control pills? Perhaps the person would prefer not to reveal such information for personal reasons but is not sure whether these drugs could cause a positive result. Such individuals are placed in an embarrassing, if not humiliating, position.

Relation to Actual Performance (Validity of Tests). Tests must give information relevant to the requirements of the job in order to be considered valid. The validity of curent drug-testing procedures is highly questionable (Kupfer 1988; Maltby 1990; Vodanovich and Reyna 1988). For one thing, the tests do not discriminate between casual use and habitual abuse and therefore do not determine whether the employee is currently impaired.

For instance, an employee who smoked marijuana three weeks previously at a Saturday night party may test positive because marijuana stays in the system up to a month. Meanwhile, another employee currently experiencing severe cocaine withdrawal may test negative because all traces of the drug can completely leave the system in about three days (Kupfer 1988). Which employee would most likely be able to perform his or her job duties responsibly? Put another way, suppose these employees are airline pilots, and one of them is going to fly the plane you are boarding. Which one would you rather have at the controls? If the airline uses urinalysis as its chosen method to detect drug use among employees, an impaired pilot may end up flying the plane while an unimpaired pilot is grounded.

Research has been contradictory on the effects of drugs on performance in the workplace. A study by the U.S. Postal Service confirmed a link between drug use (testing positive in pre-employment screening) and risk of accidents, injuries, and absenteeism, although the increase in risk was much smaller than the previous evidence had indicated ("Postal Study" 1990; Winslow 1990). However, a U.S. Department of Labor study has failed to document conclusively that drugs undercut productivity and other aspects of the work relationship (Human Resource Management News, 1990b).

Privacy and Invasiveness. As discussed previously, drug testing can be seen as an invasion of privacy, especially with the more invasive procedures. Urine samples, for instance, are not absolutely controlled unless a second party actually views the person being tested voiding into a bottle (Greenberg 1990). Health information that an employee or potential employee may not wish to share with anyone other than a personal physician may need to be shared with company personnel in order to avoid the brand of "drug user." Related to this is the fear that such information may not remain confidential once the company learns of it. This fear in most cases may be groundless, but perception is reality for the employee; if the fear is present, the employee is likely to feel abused.

Ineffectiveness of Drug Testing Programs. It is frequently claimed that drug testing can improve a company's productivity through decreased absenteeism, accident rates and so forth. Unfortunately, the evidence for such claims is often methodologically flawed. For instance, Vodanovich and Reyna (1988) cite a company that attributed its decreased accident rate to drug testing, ignoring the already established trend of decreasing accident rates in the years preceding the drug testing program as well as a company safety program initiated during the program. A company that begins drug testing frequently will also roll out an educational campaign about the program and about drugs and their impact, so that employees will understand why the company has decided to do the testing. Rarely is it possible to separate the effects of the testing program from the effects of the educational program.

Given these problems with invasive types of drug testing, why do companies do it? Once again, one must return to the basic problem for which drug testing has become a solution. Is the company trying to avoid performance impairment associated with drug use? Or is it trying to avoid having employees who use drugs on the payroll? Do employers really have the right to control what employees do on their own time? In a democratic society, the answer to this can be yes only if what they do on their own time impairs their performance at work. The real issue then becomes clear. In order to ensure that performance at work is not impaired, there are far better methods than testing urine or blood for the presence of illegal drugs.

Alternatives to Drug Testing

Performance testing is one method that has recently begun to be used as an alternative to drug testing. One company that uses it employs drivers of sightseeing buses (Maltby 1990). Every morning when the drivers report to work, they take a performance test by playing a specialized kind of video game for approximately thirty seconds. If a driver's concentration or coordination is impaired, this test will pick it up. If the driver passes the test, he or she is competent to drive that day. Drivers that fail may be sent home or assigned to nondriving duties for that day. This is one of a variety of performance tests that use video screens to test eye-hand coordination. These tests require considerable concentration and often practice. In one test currently on the market, employees perform the test a number of times to establish their own personal baseline. The computer stores this baseline information and measures each employee against his or her own baseline average each time the employee performs the test (Hamilton 1991).

Not only is performance testing noninvasive, it also gives immediate results and measures the ability to do the job. Granted, by measuring only current impairment, it cannot distinguish its cause (i.e., drugs, alcohol, emotional stress, fatigue, illness), but a positive result with urinalysis cannot distinguish whether the employee ingested an illegal substance or prescribed drug, much less when—an hour before or a month before—the employee may have ingested it. If an employee must be confronted, it is far better to confront on the basis of performance, which is clearly job related, than on the basis of urine or blood testing, which is not. This is also far safer, from the standpoint of liability. Another benefit of such an approach is that it is more likely than drug testing to be paired with a corrective rather than a punishing approach.

This method of detecting worker impairment is growing in popularity (Milbank and Rigdon 1991). Evidence for its effectiveness is promising. One company that has been using performance testing for a year reports a 67 percent decrease in accidents, a 92 percent decrease in errors, and a 64 percent decrease in workers' compensation claims. More research is needed, however, before these decreases can be attributed with confidence to performance testing alone. Such claims may in fact suffer from the same flawed methodology cited above for drug testing—that is, what else changed at the time performance testing was implemented? Was an educational program about the testing begun as well? If so, did it contain information about drug use and safety? Even if these documented health and safety improvements cannot be attributed solely to the performance testing program, there are other reasons for its superiority over drug testing, namely, that it tests current impairment and fitness for work, and that the results are directly job related.

Why haven't more companies embraced performance testing rather than the far riskier alternative of invasive bodily fluid analysis? Perhaps it is still too new a technology and many companies have not yet learned about it. If so, we may see an abandonment of blood and urine drug testing in favor of performance testing. However, the possibility remains that some companies are more interested in controlling their employees' private lives. Murphy (1988) has warned about the pressures upon managers to find out what employees do outside of work and to use the threat of job discipline or job loss to control how they live their lives, regardless of whether those choices have a specific effect on job performance.

Companies that practice those techniques may resist the notion of performance testing.

Other reasons lead companies to turn to drug testing to combat drug use. To fully understand this behavior, refer to Chapter 4's discussion on punishment and aversive control strategies. Because of our society's reliance on punishment as a method of behavior control, ineffective as it is, this strategy is turned to first when behavior problems arise in the workforce. Given the severity of the drug abuse problem in this country, managers and decision makers in companies understandably want to do something about it. As Pace and Smits (1989) point out, this desire often leads to wanting to catch and punish offenders, because managers believe that quick, decisive action paired with harsh penalties is warranted and demanded by the severity of the problem. The company therefore concentrates on a search to identify the guilty employees and punish them, expecting that the visibility of the negative consequences will frighten the employee body into discontinuing drug use.

However, as was demonstrated in Chapter 4, punishment is a very ineffective strategy for changing behavior. A punishment-oriented drug testing program most likely will fail in its goal of reducing drug use. Does this mean that companies should abandon all methods of detecting drug abuse within their employee bodies? No—this merely means that a program based on a model of finding and punishing offenders, in addition to being an example of employee abuse, will be less successful than a program based on a more integrated model that combines a rehabilitative approach with prevention-oriented strategies. An overreliance on the testing portion of such an approach, according to Pace and Smits (1989) leads to a "simplistic, faddish approach to drug testing as a cure-all." If drug testing is to be used at all, they suggest, it needs to be part of an overall system of employee assistance and concern for people and their right to privacy. It must include preventive management and proactive measures such as structuring and running an employee assistance program like a business, defining treatment and cost-management objectives for the employee assistance program and avoiding fads and simplistic solutions to the complex issue of substance abuse at work. Vodanovich and Reyna (1988) suggest a model with three components: education, treatment, and behavior (performance testing). As one executive pointed out, "If all you do is drug testing, if you don't train your supervisors to spot problems, or promote your employee assistance program, or communicate clearly and sympathetically with your employees, then you don't have a drug program" (Kupfer 1988). Fortunately, less than 9 percent of surveyed companies depend on testing alone to combat drug abuse (Zetlin 1991).

HONESTY TESTING

Employee theft is a growing problem in some businesses and a serious potential concern for all employers. Although it is difficult to obtain accurate estimates of the amount of employee theft that occurs, some estimates do exist. A figure of $40 billion for annual losses to U.S. businesses from nonviolent crimes has been cited by various sources (Clark and Hollinger 1983; Zemke 1990). Nonviolent crimes include employee theft, vandalism, and bribery. These problems have given rise to a strong desire among employers to screen out individuals who would be likely to engage in such acts. Thus, the interest in finding appropriate screening tools has grown. With the lie detector test having been barred from use as a screening tool, employers have turned to less invasive ways to test the honesty of employees and potential job applicants.

One method used to determine honesty is a questionnaire that asks people what they would do in certain situations. These tests are being used to weed out individuals who might have a propensity to steal from the company. Unfortunately, validity is not clearly demonstrated for many of these instruments. Critics cite a number of problems with these tests: certain questions are overly intrusive; tests may discriminate against minorities; test publishers are overly zealous in their claims about what the tests can accomplish (e.g., increased productivity, lower turnover rates, higher profits); and tests don't account for how a person's propensity to steal might change depending on circumstances (Fuchsberg 1990).

The Office of Technology Assessment released a report in fall 1990 unfavorable to integrity testing (U.S. Congress 1990), and the American Psychological Association (APA) has made major qualifications regarding their use (APA 1991). The APA task force report found that honesty tests varied enormously in their compliance with standards regarding validity. Publishers of honesty tests also were highly variable with regard to the amount of information that they made available to substantiate their claims of validity and utility. Most publishers are wary of publishing information concerning the development of their honesty tests, their structure and content, and their scoring keys, appealing to the proprietary nature of such information. Without access to this information, it is impossible for "a qualified reviewer to determine whether applicable standards were met" ("Standards" 1985). The task force did find that for those few tests for which validity information is available, the evidence supports their predictive validity. However, it also stated that "the information available even from the most open of the publishers would not permit an outside reviewer to judge whether the use of their test meets some specific *Standards*" (p. 10).

Although the APA report has been cited widely as supporting the validity of honesty testing, upon closer examination one has to wonder whether the writers of such reviews actually have read the report. The statements in the report that support the validity and use of honesty tests are heavily qualified. The task force was clearly disappointed with the available information on honesty tests and was not persuaded by the claims of "proprietary" material. It urged all honesty test publishers to "make available to qualified parties complete and detailed reports of research on their tests, including all negative findings." The strongest statement of support in its report was that it did not believe there is any sound basis for prohibiting the development and use of honesty tests, especially because to do so would only invite less desirable forms of pre-employment screening that would be less available for professional scrutiny. This is hardly an endorsement of the methodology.

The report also issued some strong reservations about current practices with regard to honesty testing. It strongly discouraged the use of "cutting scores" to divide test takers into two (pass versus fail) or three (high, medium, and low risk) categories, a practice that currently is standard in business and that the test manuals encourage. The report also urged the development of more comprehensive procedures for training test users, for ensuring that only qualified persons administer and interpret the tests, for educating test users about alternative selection methods, and for safeguarding the confidentiality, privacy, and informed consent of all applicants.

Given the extensive concerns that the APA has documented, it becomes even more important that these tests be administered and interpreted only by qualified professionals—an extremely rare occurrence in the corporate setting. These tests are simply not a practical tool at this time for most companies to use in order to screen out undesirables. Companies that use them risk branding honest individuals as potential thieves while failing to identify the truly dishonest individuals.

Companies would be well advised to put more time and energy into understanding the motivations and aspirations of their employees, how their own corporate culture affirms or denies those aspirations, and what kinds of behavior their own reward systems—both formal and informal— promote. Using an integrity test to select only honest people and then treating employees as if they were incompetent, lazy, opportunistic, and untrustworthy will never fail to produce the behavior that was presumably screened out in the first place. How employees are treated (or how they perceive they are treated) can give far more insight into potential lost profits than can a written integrity test.

OTHER PSYCHOLOGICAL TESTING

Personality Testing

Many instruments are available that can provide insight into certain aspects of personality. Most that are backed up by solid research have some limitations on their use. For instance, only licensed professional psychologists can obtain them and use them. However, some instruments have fewer restrictions on their use or none at all. Many of these are not well validated, some are based on questionable theoretical premises about the structure of personality, and none was meant to be used as the sole instrument of assessment. Most were not intended to be true personality tests, in the sense of an in-depth psychological assessment.

Many of these tests have come into vogue as team-building, selection, or development tools. However, in the hands of nonprofessionals, these tests can be misunderstood and misused. There is the danger of stereotyping individuals on the basis of a faulty instrument, incomplete understanding of a valid instrument, or inadequate assessment procedures. Such stereotyping can lead to limitations of career options, or even termination of employment.

One of the most popular of these instruments is the Myers-Briggs Type Indicator (MBTI). Over two million people took this test in 1990, according to its publisher (Lee 1991). This test is described by its developers as a test of "preferences," not a personality test. Based on Carl Jung's personality theory of opposite tendencies within the psyche, it is a useful way of describing the various ways that people perceive the world and make decisions. The MBTI determines one's preferences on four scales, with two categories in each scale: extraversion-introversion (E or I), sensing-intuitive (S or N), thinking-feeling (T or F), and perceiving-judging (P or J). Thus, there are sixteen possible types, indicated by four-letter combinations (e.g., ISTJ). This test can give useful feedback about one's own preferences. Used in a team context, it can yield data about the preferences of one's co-workers, bosses, and subordinates.

The operative word here is *preferences*. The theory behind the test never states that an individual cannot behave in ways other than what the test indicates is his or her preferred style. This subtle distinction seems to escape the notice of many managers who come into contact with it. There is a tendency to label people according to their type and thereby justify one's own prejudices (Lee 1991). After a brief exposure to the instrument, one middle-level manager began justifying his biases against those whose styles were different from his own. He actually told one of his opposite-typed subordinates that most of the officers of the company were of his own type, and implied that the subordinate's style would limit his advancement. This same manager, while interviewing a candidate for a job, said that he himself was one type, whereas several other people in the group were the opposite type, "so it's no wonder we don't get along."

An inadequate understanding of the MBTI often results in managers thinking that certain types are better than others. Although the theory does say that some types will be more attracted to certain kinds of work than will other types, and that some types may find certain kinds of work easier or more difficult, there is nothing in the theory that says that certain types are incapable of certain kinds of work. In fact, the promoters of the test take special pains to clarify the uses and misuses of the test when training its users. Stereotyping people and their abilities is a clear misuse of the test. Using the test as the sole criterion to determine the fit between an employee and a job is another misuse. Yet many managers, who have no training in the use of the instrument, actually make placement decisions and judgments about employees' capabilities based on test results. Even if they are not using the MBTI as the sole criterion, their lack of training in how to use the instrument argues against their using it at all for these purposes. Attendance at a workshop in which the participants use the instruments to determine their own type and understand others' types does not constitute training in the use of the instrument. One midlevel manager, after attending a course in which using a short form of the instrument was one activity, considered himself an expert in its use. This manager had no training in psychology, test theory, or any related discipline, but he began assigning work on the basis of his perceptions of subordinates' MBTI types. He even stated to one subordinate that it was necessary to be a certain type in order to do the kind of work done in his group. Needless to say, not only were his perceptions incorrect, he was also wrong in his understanding of the theory. All in all, his use of this tool was dangerous and unethical, resulting in a truly abusive situation in which his misguided perceptions and personal biases had a negative impact on the careers of some very talented people.

This discussion is not meant to be an indictment of the MBTI or any other tool meant to measure various aspects of personality or behavior. All of these can be very useful tools when used appropriately with a trained facilitator. Unfortunately, in the case of the MBTI, even though the professionals who have licensed the test have taken pains to ensure that unauthorized practitioners do not have access to it, they have been unable to prevent a certain amount of abuse of their guidelines. The test that they have licensed and over which they have control is the full form of the instrument. Even if unauthorized people were to gain access to the test booklet itself and duplicate it, they would be unable to score it. The scoring methodology is limited in distribution to those who are certified in its use. There are, however, shorter forms of the test that are unlicensed, and they are often used in corporate settings by unauthorized people. Even if the people who use it in these settings are qualified, the distribution of the test itself is not controlled. The short forms often come with simple scoring instructions that can easily be duplicated on the nearest copy machine, thus enabling people who are untrained to use and abuse it.

The primary rationale for using instruments that type people is to create awareness (Lee 1991). This awareness may be directed at knowing one's own personal style or strengths and weaknesses, or it may be directed at understanding the differences among people. This is an admirable goal. The important questions for managers and human resource professionals to answer are: Do the managers have enough training to understand and use these instruments appropriately? What are the aspects of this corporate culture that may drive managers to use them inappropriately? If the culture values technical knowledge more than knowledge about people, if there is an atmosphere of mistrust, if the company currently is experiencing turmoil and downsizing, such tools could be used, even unintentionally, as instruments of abuse.

Handwriting Analysis

Due to persistent business problems that employers would like to attribute to individual personality differences, employers' interest in selection tools has increased. Methods such as handwriting analysis, never used extensively in this country, are experiencing a resurgence of interest, especially since the ban of the lie detector for employment screening. Handwriting analysis is even less well validated than the lie detector or honesty testing but is beginning to be used by employers desperate to make selection decisions according to *some* criteria.

The theory behind handwriting analysis is that the strokes of an individual's handwriting are subconscious expressions of personality, and that studying handwriting will therefore reveal the intricacies of a personality ("Graphology" 1990; Rawlinson 1989). As a technique of analysis it is categorized as a "projective" technique, along with some well-known psychological tests like the Rorschach inkblot test. That is, rather than scoring a subject's answers on objective questions, like the previously discussed honesty tests, the test scorer interprets the subject's unstructured responses. Inferences are made concerning the subject's personality traits. The APA recognizes projective techniques in clinical and therapeutic environments but not in the job testing area (Sinai and Mazzuca 1988).

Although handwriting analysis, or graphology, has never been validated scientifically, one measure of its growing acceptance in corporate circles is that articles on handwriting analysis have recently appeared in professional human resource publications (e.g., Kurtz 1991; Taylor and Sackheim 1988). In addition to employment screening, Kurtz lobbied for its use in promotion evaluation, stress management, relocation suitability, white-collar crime detection, negotiations, management-team and employee compatibility, and strategic planning.

Estimates vary as to the number of businesses that currently use graphology as a selection tool. In Europe, an estimated 85 percent of companies use the method to evaluate and understand individual traits and to hire new personnel (Levy 1979; Sinai and Mazzuca 1988). In this country, one estimate is that between 2,000 and 2,500 employers are using graphology as part of their employee selection procedure (Rawlinson 1989).

Acceptance among nonprofessionals does not mean respectability, and graphology is not considered to have any validity among psychologists for any use. There has been very little objective study of graphology. When the methodology began to increase in popularity in business circles, some psychologists attempted to remedy the dearth of research available. Klimoski and Rafaeli (1983) concluded that the use of graphology in applied settings is premature, and that the general trend of findings shows that graphology is not a viable assessment tool. Since then little has changed. Most studies have demonstrated little or no validity for graphology (e.g., Rafaeli and Klimoski 1983; Furnham and Gunter 1987; Eysenck and Gudjonsson 1986). Neter and Ben-Shakhar (1989) found that graphologists were no better than nongraphologists in predicting future performance on the basis of handwriting samples, and, furthermore, that psychologists with no knowledge in graphology outperformed graphologists on all dimensions.

Unfortunately, people are not as simple and consistent as graphologists would claim. Companies that use handwriting analysis to aid in decision making about peoples' skills, talents, or psychological characteristics are putting themselves at great risk.

SUMMARY

The value of workplace testing is as an adjunct to the management process, not a substitute. Even psychologists who use psychological tests in their daily work retain a healthy respect for their limitations. When management decisions are based primarily on the results of tests, faulty decisions will be made.

The testing issue is an example of trying to find easy solutions to complex problems. Companies are placing far too much reliance on testing to help them solve business problems. Clearly companies face some major business problems today, some of which intersect with social problems. Competitiveness, productivity, profitability, dishonesty, and theft are all serious issues. However, before solutions are chosen, it is a good idea to determine the root causes of all of these problems. There is a strong likelihood that, from a total quality perspective, many of the root causes will be found in the business process itself. Policies, practices, traditional methods, management style, lack of employee involvement in problem solving, and a host of other factors all will affect a company's performance. If these systemic issues are part of the problem, weeding out "problem" employees will not solve it. A far better strategy would be to work on the systemic solutions first and on an ongoing basis. The selection problem then may end up being a much more limited and manageable problem, and the testing that is done will be far less likely to result in employee abuse.

REFERENCES

APA Task Force on the Prediction of Dishonesty and Theft in Employment Settings. 1991. *Questionnaires used in the prediction of trustworthiness in pre-employment selection decisions: An A.P.A. task force report.* Washington, D.C.: A.P.A. Science Directorate.

Big questions on drugs and the workplace. 1990. *Human Resource Management News* (August 25): 3–4.

Clark, J. P. and Hollinger, R. C. 1983. *Theft by employees in work organizations.* Washington, D.C.: National Institute of Justice.

Conte, C. 1991. Labor Letter. *Wall Street Journal* (March 19): A1.

Eysenck, H. J. and Gudjonsson, G. H. 1986. An empirical study of the validity of handwriting analysis. *Personality and Individual Differences* 7 (2): 263–64.

Feinstein, S. 1990. Labor Letter. *Wall Street Journal* (August 7): 1.

Fuchsberg, G. 1990. Integrity-test firms fear report card by Congress. *Wall Street Journal* (September 20): B1.

Furnham, A. and Gunter, B. 1987. Graphology and personality: Another failure to validate graphological analysis. *Personality and Individual Differences* 8 (3): 433–35.

Gold, D. and Unger, B. 1991. Check these points before using credit checks. *HR News* (June): A6.

Graphology: The power of the written word. 1990. *The Economist* (June 16): 97–98.

Greenberg, E. R. 1990. Workplace testing: The 1990 AMA survey, part 2. *Personnel* (July): 26–29.

Hamilton, J.O.C. 1991. A video game that tells if employees are fit for work. *Business Week* (June 3): 36.

Klimoski, R. J. and Rafaeli, A. 1983. Inferring personal qualities through handwriting analysis. *Journal of Occupational Psychology* 56: 191–202.

Kupfer, A. 1988. Is drug testing good or bad? *Fortune* (December 19): 133–39.

Kurtz, S. 1991. Screening employees for the "write" stuff: Graphology in the workplace. *The Human Resources Professional* (Winter): 52–57.

Lee, C. 1991. What's your style? *Training* (May): 27–33.

Levy, L. 1979. Handwriting and hiring. *Dun's Review* 113: 72–79.

Maltby, L. L. 1990. Put performance to the test. *Personnel* (July): 30–31.

Milbank, D. and Rigdon, J. E. 1991. Labor letter. *Wall Street Journal* (January 29): 1.

More firms testing workers for drugs. 1991. *San Francisco Chronicle* (March 19): C2.

Murphy, J. A. 1988. Whose business is it? Your job and your privacy. *Vital Speeches of the Day* (December 15): 146–49.

Neter, E. and Ben-Shakhar, G. 1989. The predictive validity of graphological inferences: A meta-analytic approach. *Personality and Individual Differences* 10 (7): 737–45.

Pace, L. A. and Smits, S. J. 1989. When managers are substance abusers. *Personnel Journal* (July): 70–72.

Poe, R. and Baker, E. L. 1990. Fast forward. *Across the Board* (May): 7–8.

Postal study links drug use and job. 1990. *Human Resource Management News* (December 22): 3–4.

Rafaeli, A. and Klimoski, R. J. 1983. Predicting sales success through handwriting analysis: An evaluation of the effects of training and handwriting sample content. *Journal of Applied Psychology* 68 (2): 212–17.

Rawlinson, H. 1989. Pre-employment testing. *Small Business Reports* (April): 20–27.

Sinai, L. and Mazzuca, L. 1988. Written tests not always valid: Lawyers. *Business Insurance* (September 19): 19–22.

Standards for educational and psychological testing. 1985. Washington, D.C.: American Psychological Association.

Taylor, M. S. and Sackheim, K. K. 1988. Graphology. *Personnel Administrator* (May): 71–76.

U.S. Congress, Office of Technology Assessment. 1990. *The use of integrity tests for pre-employment screening*. Washington, D.C.: U.S. Government Printing Office.

Vodanovich, S. J. and Reyna, M. 1988. Alternatives to workplace testing. *Personnel Administrator* (May): 78–84.

Winslow, R. 1990. Study may spur job-applicant drug screening. *Wall Street Journal* (November 28): B1.

Zemke, E. 1990. Do honesty tests tell the truth? *Training* (October): 75–81.

Zetlin, M. 1991. Corporate America declares war on drugs. *Personnel* (August): 1.

9

Potential for New Forms of Abuse: Employee Privacy

Employee privacy is becoming a controversial and explosive issue. The Conference Board characterizes the issue as a collision between a company's need for employee information and individual privacy rights (Alster 1990). The American Civil Liberties Union (ACLU) takes the position that individual freedom today is endangered more by employers than by government (Rankin 1990). In 1990 the ACLU mounted a campaign to extend to the U.S. workplace the freedoms guaranteed by the Constitution's Bill of Rights. This organization is concerned about employers engaging in electronic spying, monitoring employees' personal telephone calls, using hidden cameras, keeping secret records of employees' computer habits, forcing employees to answer deeply probing psychological tests, and requiring cholesterol tests or drug tests as a prerequisite to keeping one's job.

The president of a major U.S. company has stated publicly that managers are being pressed to snoop into employees' private lives and to threaten firing or job discipline to control their private behavior, whether or not that behavior affects job performance (Murphy 1988). He includes in this assessment such things as random drug tests, random AIDS tests, electronic eavesdropping, and pulmonary function tests, and he makes the direct assertion that these tests are being done in most cases not to diagnose specific performance problems, but "to check up indiscriminately on how people live their lives outside of work" (p. 147). Evidence of such efforts to control employees' lives comes from organizations like the ACLU, which has documented instances such as one in which a company fired two long-time employees solely because they refused to quit smoking cigarettes in their own homes (Rankin 1990).

Organizations such as the ACLU, 9 to 5, (an organization representing office workers), and labor unions are becoming increasingly vocal about privacy in the workplace. Although these groups do not oppose such practices as electronic monitoring when it is done to train employees and provide them with direct performance feedback (Reynolds 1991), they do oppose what they perceive as excessive dependence on electronic measurements, leading to widespread abuses of employees and unnecessary, humiliating invasions of privacy. They cite cases (Allen 1991b; Murray 1991) such as:

- An employee being fired because of something said while on a personal telephone call;

- A recruiter being harangued unnecessarily because he made fewer telephone calls than his colleagues even though he got good results;

- An employer timing and posting employees' visits to the bathroom;

- An employee whose boss cut her salary in half after eavesdropping on her calls, explaining "I hear you talk to all those men friends of yours, and besides, you have that rich uncle—let them pay for some of your bills."

In addition to the privacy concerns themselves, another concern for human resource managers in particular is the widespread ignorance within the human resource field about state regulations affecting employees' privacy. A survey by the Society for Human Resource Management ("Employee Privacy" 1991) showed that, of surveyed managers: more than half did not know if their states had laws on the surveillance of employee activities in the workplace; more than half were unaware of the conditions under which employees' records could be disclosed, and to whom; and more than one-third did not know if their state regulated an employee's access to his or her own personnel file, the collection of information about employees, or substance abuse testing. To the extent that human resource managers are unaware of the regulations surrounding issues of privacy in the workplace, policy decisions around these issues may put their companies at risk. Furthermore, any advice that they provide to other managers in the business may be inaccurate, potentially jeopardizing employee privacy rights and contributing to abusive management practices.

CREDIT REPORTING

Many companies buy credit reports on prospective employees in an effort to judge their integrity. They believe that knowing how an applicant handles personal finances helps predict whether he or she is likely to behave dishonestly or irresponsibly in the workplace (Fritz 1990). These reports are being used to screen personnel for all types of jobs, even those that do not involve handling money. Although the law requires that the applicant be informed if his or her credit report contributes to not being selected for the job, frequently this information is not shared with the applicant (Fritz 1990; Fuchsberg 1990; Overman 1991). Disclosure is required even if the credit report information played only a small part in the decision to reject the applicant. If credit reports are used as part of a decision involving current employees (e.g., a job transfer or termination), this disclosure requirement also applies. The employee must be informed that credit report information was obtained, and the name and address of the credit bureau making the report must be disclosed as well.

Several issues involved in the use of credit reports relate to employee abuse. First, although employers who use these reports claim they have predictive validity for on-the-job behavior, there is no evidence linking poor credit histories to dishonesty or poor job performance (Fritz 1990). Honest people can experience financial difficulties that result in a poor credit rating, and people with excellent credit ratings sometimes cannot resist temptation.

Second, credit reports often contain inaccuracies (e.g., Miller 1991). Unless a credit report is confirmed to be accurate, employment, advancement, or development could be denied to someone based on false information about his or her personal finances. It is a safe assumption that companies that do not inform applicants or employees that credit report information contributed to a decision also do not verify the accuracy of the reports with the individuals. Given that such selection decisions are made based on a variety of factors, there is no reason to believe that someone who is rejected for a job, a transfer, or a promotion would automatically think that credit information played a part in the decision. This situation points up a final issue: it might be very difficult for an individual to find out that a credit report was used if the company does not inform him or her. The law permits individuals to sue employers for actual damages suffered from a Fair Credit Report Act violation that occurs because of negligence, as well as for punitive damages if it is established that the employer willfully violated the law (Overman 1991). However, the right to sue may be meaningless, given how difficult it may be to establish whether and how credit reports were used.

ELECTRONIC MONITORING

As computer technology makes available new ways to speed service and increase output, it also increases the ease of electronically keeping track of service and productivity indicators. Employers now have the capability to count the number of keystrokes typed on word processors and to listen in on the telephone calls of telemarketing staff, reservation clerks, insurance claim processors, and telephone operators. Unions as well as other organizations representing employee interests, such as the ACLU and 9 to 5, are concerned about potential and actual abuses of such monitoring and are lobbying for legal and legislative remedies.

Among the employee abuse issues involved in electronic monitoring are the following:

- Whether the monitoring is done secretly or employees are informed when monitoring is occurring.
- Electronic monitoring's contribution to stress.
- The purposes of electronic monitoring: training, discipline, evaluation of performance, and setting unrealistically high performance goals.

Legislation is currently pending that would restrict electronic monitoring in the following ways:

- Employers would be required to notify employees of any electronic monitoring that may directly affect them with signals (lights or tones) when monitoring is taking place.
- Employers would be prohibited from collecting personal information not related to an employee's work performance.
- Employers would be prohibited from using electronic monitoring data as the only basis for performance evaluation or disciplinary action (Reynolds 1991; Messmer 1991).

The Communications Workers of America (CWA) has been very active in lobbying against uncontrolled secret monitoring. Telephone operators in one of the locals represented by CWA have identified monitoring as the number-one pressure in their job (Murray 1991). The union explains that it is the secret nature of the monitoring that is most distressing to employees, especially when they cannot even see the supervisor doing the monitoring because they may be in another building. Not all of the CWA's members are subjected to undisclosed monitoring, however. Pacific Bell, for instance, uses a light to indicate when supervisors are listening to operators' calls, so that the operators know when monitoring is going on (Murray 1991).

Electronic monitoring, especially when done in secret, has been linked to increased work-related stress, illness, and injury (Baker 1990). A study done in connection with CWA (Smith et al. 1990), showed that telecommunications workers who are electronically monitored have greater health problems than nonmonitored workers. This study has been criticized on methodological grounds due to a low response rate (762 responses out of 2,900 surveyed). However, it is the first major study to investigate systematically the relationship between electronic monitoring and employee health and well-being, and the results confirm the pattern of anecdotal evidence that has been mounting over the years since electronic monitoring began.

Effectiveness of Electronic Monitoring

With all of this electronic monitoring going on, it would be easy to assume that it is being done to improve productivity. It seems clear that one of the motivations is probably management's belief that it can improve productivity. Does it, though? None of the arguments for or against monitoring have considered whether it is effective. The focus has been on efficiency (e.g., time spent per call), not effectiveness, from the company's point of view, and there is an implicit assumption that monitoring is an effective technique for increasing productivity. Part of the role of human resource professionals must be to get organizations to concentrate on effectiveness rather than efficiency.

Some service leaders have decided that electronic monitoring not only does not improve productivity but actually causes service indicators to deteriorate. It is necessary to think beyond speed of service and concentrate on other aspects, such as quality. Federal Express, Bell Canada, USAA, and Northwest Airlines have all either begun to stress quality over quantity or have abandoned monitoring altogether. *Business Week* publicized how these companies have emphasized service over speed with the following case histories (Bernstein 1991).

Federal Express, in response to competitive threats in 1984, began to emphasize speed in handling calls. It began to monitor the length of time customer service agents spent on each call, and speed of handling comprised 50 percent of an agent's performance review. Feedback from the agents told the company that limiting the length of calls to 140 seconds resulted in two negative effects: it created too much stress, and it made them cut off customers before their questions were answered. The company's response was to institute a new system. Now, a supervisor listens in on a random call twice a year, then sits down with the agent for a discussion focusing on quality. The length of calls is not even mentioned in this discussion. The most intriguing effect of this change is that, not only have employees' and executives' perceptions of service improved, but the average call length dropped to 135 seconds.

Bell Canada reports a similar experience. Like most communications companies, Bell Canada had been electronically monitoring its operators' calls and was facing union opposition to the practice. In addition, top management was growing increasingly concerned about quality. A six-month trial was instituted in which operators were monitored as a group, instead of individually, on the speed of calls. When the group average increased, management asked the operators what the cause might have been and worked with them to get the average back down. The trial was a success: productivity stayed up, operators' perceptions of service improved, and job satisfaction increased. Because of the success of the trial, all of Bell Canada's operators now work under this new system.

One of the best ways to stimulate performance improvement is merely to post results. The information alone seems to enable people to improve. One reason is that the information serves a reinforcing function. People can get feedback about their improvements in a timely way. But monitoring carries with it the baggage of surveillance and supervisors checking up on employees; if it could be used to provide only feedback, it might work the way it is supposed to. In this case supervisors would have to be kept out of the picture or use only group results. In any case, employee involvement would be necessary to determine the parameters around monitoring and how to use the results.

SURVEILLANCE: SPYING ON EMPLOYEES

Advances in technology beyond electronic monitoring have made it easier to conduct surveillance on employees. In some instances, electronic surveillance has been used in the workplace to monitor nonwork activities as well as work activities. One case of workers who had discovered hidden video cameras in all company bathrooms came to the attention of the ACLU (Rankin 1990).

A different kind of surveillance was used when the office of a top security official at General Dynamics Corporation was bugged (Wartzman and Stevens 1991). The target of the surveillance device suspected a fellow employee but claimed that higher-level managers stonewalled his attempts to follow up on the incident. A former lawyer for General Dynamics has sued the company, claiming that he was wrongfully dismissed for attempting to get to the bottom of the bugging incident among other things.

Security experts say that executives and managers often overreact when they discover that internal information is being leaked to sources outside the company. They often must convince these managers to stay within the legal bounds in fighting such incidents. The development of increasingly sophisticated electronic monitoring devices may allow competitors to listen in illegally, but they also provide opportunities to use illegal or unethical means to try to stop such leaks. One security expert related that he has had to try to convince executives that they cannot legally bug their own employees, and even if they could do so legally, they would risk a lawsuit (Allen 1991a).

Procter & Gamble discovered, to its dismay, that using technology in an attempt to plug a leak can backfire. In a well-publicized incident, Procter & Gamble attempted to discover the source of a news leak of some secret corporate plans. Through the police and a court subpoena of telephone records, the company tried to identify the person who had called a Pittsburgh-based *Wall Street Journal* reporter from the Cincinnati area (Schneidawind 1991). This incident created a public relations nightmare for Procter & Gamble, prompting the company to abort the search and the chairman to apologize to employees in a letter.

ELECTRONIC MAIL

Electronic mail systems (E-mail), in which employees can send messages to others directly through a personal computer, have become a standard mode of communication at many companies. Serious issues of privacy have arisen as people have tested the limits of these systems. E-mail messages must loop through a central, company-owned computer. That makes it possible for a manager, with a little motivation and some computer knowledge, to access E-mail messages sent to other employees. In one much-publicized case, an employee at Epson America, Inc., discovered that her supervisor had put a tap on the E-mail system and was reading both internal messages and correspondence between employees and people outside the company (Reese 1990). The employee herself sent a message to someone else calling her supervisor a "boneheaded tyrant" (Maney 1991). When she blew the whistle on her supervisor's unauthorized surveillance of communications that had been presumed to be private, she was fired for insubordination, the proof of which was in her monitored messages.

Opinion varies over whether such electronic communications should be considered private and whether employers have the right to access communications sent through these systems. One argument holds that electronic data are equivalent to speech and should receive the same constitutional protection that speech and print receive. This argument has been put forth by Laurence Tribe, a distinguished professor of constitutional law at Harvard ("Free Speech" 1991). There are, in fact, some legal protections currently existing that protect electronic communications from electronic eavesdropping by outside third parties. The Electronic Communications Privacy Act of 1986 protects electronic communications in the same way that wiretap laws protect voice communications over the telephone (Ulrich 1991). But some have contended that this law was written before there was such a prevalent use of E-mail and is not explicit enough (Reese 1990). The controversy appears to center over the definition of "outside third parties." Is the company that owns the electronic mail system an outside third party, or does it have the right to access messages because it owns the system? This question brings us to the argument, opposite to that put forth by Tribe, that since an office computer terminal and the E-mail system for which it is used belong to the employer, not the employee, all communications sent over the system also belong to the employer. Being company property, the messages sent over the E-mail system cannot and should not be considered private. The employer has the right to examine all contents of the system (e.g., Cox 1990; Reese 1990).

Because of the controversy over privacy, employers have been urged to maintain a consistent and clearly stated policy. The best approach, says one expert, is for employers not to inspect E-mail routinely, but if they do, to make that clear to employees so that they will not assume their messages are confidential (Reese 1990).

One company that decided to give such notification to avoid potential liability inserted a message on the E-mail system that appears on a screen every time an employee logs on. This message informs employees that the system is company property, is to be used only for work-related purposes, and is subject to inspection. Because this new screen appeared suddenly and without explanation, its appearance generated a storm of dialog. Questions were raised, suspicions were aroused, and motives were assumed. This incident demonstrates that it is worthwhile, before attempting such notification, to strategize about the best way to accomplish it and to involve the human resource department, in addition to the generally recognized stakeholders such as security, legal, and information services as one of the stakeholders in the decision.

VOICE MAIL

Voice mail has been hailed as a productivity-enhancing tool. No longer need employees waste valuable time playing telephone tag by trading messages via a secretary. Now questions, answers, and information can be left in a "voice mailbox" if the person is unreachable. Many employees have discovered, however, that there is also a depersonalizing aspect to voice mail that can give rise to abuse.

Insecure managers who are uncomfortable with confrontation find it easier to criticize and confront through voice mail than in person (the same is true with E-mail). Not only does the manager not have to worry about looking at the person while communicating, he or she does not have to respond immediately to the other person's reaction. It becomes relatively easy to leave a message full of negativity, criticism, and innuendo. Such a communication would be unlikely face-to-face because the other person would stop the process by speaking up. In voice mail, the interactive nature of communication is interrupted and delayed. Countless numbers of subordinates have been infuriated or mystified by messages that would never have been communicated had there not been a convenient alternative to face-to-face communication.

The subordinates of one such manager discovered that they all had experienced the same kind of abusive, harassing messages from their manager, yet they rarely, if ever, faced such negative behavior from him in person. These messages became an issue for the whole group when it confronted him about it in a staff meeting. In addition to this practice being seen as personally insulting and devaluing, it was perceived as a productivity drain. Rather than resolving a question in a two-minute face-to-face conversation, they were forced to engage in a series of voice mail exchanges, often lengthy ones. They found voice mail an ineffective method to deal with their supervisor's distorted perception and accusations and attempt to impart correct information that could alleviate his misunderstanding of a situation. In addition, the manager's threatening and abusive tone generated in his subordinates negative emotions that affected their productivity. After confronting the manager, the group came to some agreements about the limits of voice mail and about what kinds of issues for which it was appropriate and inappropriate. This manager changed his voice mail behavior, although he occasionally reverted to his abusive techniques, especially when under stress.

Other abusive aspects of voice mail stem from its ubiquity. Messages can be left and accessed twenty-four hours a day, and in some organizations employees are expected to access their voice mail messages even during off-hours. In one incident, the time of a Monday morning meeting was changed and notification was sent out over the weekend. Those who had not accessed their voice mail over the weekend were, of course, late to the meeting and were penalized for being late. There are also instances of managers leaving important messages for employees while they are out ill. Many systems will "time out" messages—after a certain length of time, if the message has not been accessed, it is erased. Sometimes this time window is relatively brief—a week or less. One manager left messages for an employee who was out on a planned surgical disability for several weeks. She did not access her messages while she was recovering from her surgery, and so she never got the information. In another instance, a manager left voice mail messages for an employee who had been admitted to the hospital for an emergency. This employee never received a telephone call from his manager inquiring about his health, but he did get several voice mail messages with requests for work to be accomplished.

These unfortunate patterns of abusive communication cannot be blamed solely on voice mail. Of course, the technology did not create these negative interpersonal styles of communication. It only provided an opportunity for such harassment to be expressed. Nevertheless, it can be argued that the availability of this technology can reinforce abusive tendencies.

SUMMARY

Technology is a double-edged sword. Along with its potential for enhancing the quality of life comes responsibility to use it in constructive ways that do not harm people. Many of the technologies that can be used today in workplace situations to enhance productivity need to be subjected to this kind of critical examination. If this does not happen, human nature being what it is, the compelling nature of such sophisticated management tools may cause people to focus more on the capability of the technology than on its human impact in the organization. Human resource managers have a major contribution to make in this area by educating management in their companies about the threats to privacy and resulting losses in productivity when such tools are misused.

REFERENCES

Allen, M. 1991a. Security experts advise firms to avoid panic, excess zeal in probing data leaks. *Wall Street Journal* (September 20): B1.

———. 1991b. Legislation could restrict bosses from snooping on their workers. *Wall Street Journal* (September 24): B1.

Alster, J., ed. 1990. Will privacy issues come to a head in the '90s? *Human Resources Briefing* (August): 3.

Baker, B. 1990. Monitoring of VDT work leads to more injuries, study says. *Los Angeles Times* (October 6): D1.

Bernstein, A. 1991. How to motivate workers: Don't watch 'em. *Business Week* (April 29): 56.

Cox, H. 1990. Workplace privacy? There isn't any. *USA Today* (September 17): 12A.

Employee privacy: A gap between action and knowledge. 1991. *Human Resource Management News* (July 15): 2–3.

Free speech and computers (Editorial). 1991. *San Francisco Examiner* (March 27): A16.

Fritz, N. R. 1990. HR Focus: More credit checks. *Personnel* (September): 5–6.

Fuchsberg, G. 1990. Managing: Use of credit reports in hiring draws a caution. *Wall Street Journal* (October 7): B1.

Maney, K. 1991. Computers do more of the talking. *USA Today* (June 26): 1B.

Messmer, E. 1991. Vendors assail privacy bill's curbs on work monitoring. *Network World* (August 5): 7.

Miller, M. W. 1991. Credit: an open book—with typos. *Wall Street Journal* (March 27): B1.

Murphy, J. A. 1988. Whose business is it? Your job and your privacy. *Vital Speeches of the Day* (December 15): 146–49.

Murray, K. 1991. Electronic monitoring of unknowing workers has been on the rise. *Orange County Register* (July 1): 1.

Overman, S. 1991. FTC agreement points out credit check abuse. *HR News* (August): 9.

Rankin, R. A. 1990. Workers' privacy seen as eroding. *San Jose Mercury News* (December 19): 1A.

Reese, S. 1990. Electronic mail raises tricky questions of privacy. *Investors Daily* (November 16): 6.

Reynolds, L. 1991. Rights groups condemn eavesdropping supervisors. *Personnel* (April): 19.

Schneidawind, J. 1991. Big brother is on the phone. *USA Today* (August 14): B1.

Smith, M. J.; Sainfort, P.; Rogers, K.; and LeGrande, D. 1990. Electronic performance monitoring and job stress in telecommunications jobs. Unpublished manuscript. University of Wisconsin, Madison, Department of Industrial Engineering and the Communications Workers of America.

Ulrich, W. E. 1991. Rights of privacy in electronic mail. *Los Angeles Times*
    (March 6): D3.
Wartzman, R. and Stevens, A. 1991. General Dynamics worker files suit over
    bugging incident in California. *Wall Street Journal* (August 16): B4.

Part III
Impact on Organizations

This section looks at how employee abuse affects the organization. Chapter 10 examines the high cost paid by organizations that allow employee abuse to occur. Costs are divided into three categories based on how directly one can measure them. The first category contains all of the direct costs incurred by the organization when employees are abused. These costs include the effects of increased stress, medical and disability costs, and legal costs. The second category of costs—deteriorating quality, poor customer relationships, increased turnover and absenteeism, and even revenge or sabotage—are more indirect but no less significant. The third category is the most indirect and therefore the most difficult to measure. In fact, since this category covers the costs of lost opportunities, it is impossible to measure, but it is potentially the most costly in terms of effectiveness, productivity, and profitability. Included as opportunity costs are the lack of discretionary effort by employees (doing only what is necessary rather than going above and beyond the call of duty), commitments outside the job, time spent talking about the problem, and loss of creativity. The opportunity that is lost is the opportunity to become a quality company, because employee abuse creates a hostile work environment. Employee involvement, discretionary effort, creativity and innovation, all necessary for quality, disappear in an environment of fear and mistrust.

Chapter 11 considers corporate programs that, while not designed to deal directly with employee abuse, can yield important information about abuse in the organization. These programs include ethics programs (corporate ombudsmen and ethics offices), employee assistance programs, wellness programs, grievance systems, and employee surveys. Each of these programs is discussed for its potential contribution to understanding employee abuse in the organization, auditing the company culture, and using the data for the purpose of continuous improvement.

10

The Costs of Employee Abuse

Employee abuse can have major bottom-line consequences. Although a hidden problem because of its unacknowledged status, various forms of employee abuse cost any large company millions of dollars in increased expenses and lost profits. The pressures that exist in companies today, and that have increased significantly in recent years, are placing enormous stress on managers and employees and are triggering abusive behavior in managers (Smith 1988). As of 1988, mental health experts estimated that up to 15 percent of executives and managers were suffering from depression or critical levels of stress that would eventually affect job performance. The most recent estimate is that stress-related problems and mental illness (including depression) is costing business $150 billion annually in health insurance and disability claims, lost productivity, and other expenses.

The costs associated with employee abuse can be grouped into three categories for discussion. The first category is the direct cost due to stress and disability claims, workers' compensation claims, increased medical costs, and lawsuits, including wrongful discharge. The second category includes more indirect costs, such as poor quality, high turnover, absenteeism, poor customer relationships, or even sabotage. Finally, there are the even more indirect "opportunity" costs of lowered employee commitment, such as lack of discretionary effort, commitments outside the job, time spent talking about the problem rather than working, and loss of creativity.

DIRECT COSTS

Stress, Disability, and Workers' Compensation

Many companies have reported skyrocketing medical claims due primarily to stress-related medical and psychological conditions. Wilson (1991) found that job pressures are cited in 75 percent of workers' compensation claims in which mental stressors were the main cause of absenteeism, and 94 percent of those claims resulted from abusive treatment of an employee by a manager (Wilson refers to it as "cumulative psychic workplace trauma"). Voluck and Abramson (1987) also have stated that the most frequently cited causes of stress involve supervisory conduct or employer action or inaction.

One consultant on corporate change estimated in 1988 that at least 45 percent of American managers suffer from too much stress, and that as a result "they are becoming abusive, intolerant, and dictatorial" (Smith 1988). The pressure-cooker environment in companies has not let up since this statement was made and has perhaps intensified in many organizations. A few years later, 45 percent of managers may be a low estimate of the number inflicting stress-induced abuse.

According to a recent Gallup survey of personnel and medical directors, 25 percent of their companies' workforces suffer from stress-related illnesses or anxiety disorders (Poe and Baker 1990). Even more recently, a study conducted by Northwestern National Life Insurance Company (NWNL) demonstrated that job stress is epidemic and is increasing. Among the findings of this survey are the following:

- Seven in ten workers say that job stress is causing frequent health problems.

- Fifty-three percent of workers are required to work more than forty hours per week very or somewhat often.

- More workers report high levels of job stress. Forty-six percent of workers say that their jobs are highly stressful. An earlier study in 1985 reported only 20 percent experiencing a high level of job stress.

- One-third of workers had seriously considered quitting their jobs during the previous year and 14 percent had actually changed jobs in the last two years due to workplace stress.

- Seventeen percent of workers reported high absenteeism due to stress (Pasternak 1991a; Scovel 1991).

In this study, the factors that caused stress most frequently were the following:

- Too much work, long hours, deadlines (28 percent)
- Working with the public or special populations such as children, prisoners, or the severely ill (25 percent)
- The boss or manager (18 percent)
- Co-workers (15 percent) (Walters et al. 1991).

One of the trends that presumably led to NWNL's survey was an increase in stress disabilities in its caseloads. Over the previous ten years, NWNL had seen a doubling of these claims. Stress claims compose the fastest-growing category of workers' compensation cases. In 1980 they accounted for 5 percent of all occupational disease claims; in 1989 this figure had risen to 15 percent (LaVan, Katz, and Hochwarter 1990). All these trends together are a powerful indication of the extent and severity of employee abuse.

Increased Medical Costs

Depression is one of the major consequences of stress, especially stress caused by employee abuse. Wilson (1991) lists depressed moods, along with anxiety and emotional outbursts, among the signs to look for in identifying abused employees. Anxiety and depression are frequently seen together in individuals. Victims of abuse are particularly vulnerable to anxiety and depression. Depression, both treated and untreated, has high costs to business and to the economy. The acting director of the National Institute of Mental Health has estimated that depressive illness cost the U.S. economy $27 billion in 1989. Of that amount, $17 billion was for worker absenteeism alone (Pasternak 1991b).

Stress can cause physical ills as well. Although this is a common-sense belief, there has been scanty evidence documenting the connection until recently. Job stress (specifically the combination of high job demands and a low degree of control over them) has been shown to be associated with hypertension ("This Week's News" 1990). People who report high levels of stress are twice as likely to develop a cold as those reporting low-stress levels (Scott 1991). This study further suggested that stress can undermine the body's defenses against infectious diseases in general, opening the possibility that high stress can contribute to increased absenteeism, lost productivity, and higher medical costs.

Animal studies have shown that stress causes faster deterioration in the areas of the brain associated with learning and memory (Buderi 1991). Nerve cells in those areas in the brain were less active in young, stressed rats than in nonstressed rats, indicating that at least temporarily, their ability to learn and remember was impaired. The additional stress sped up the actual loss of brain cells in older rats. A direct link has not been established for humans, but until it is, the researcher says, "it seems prudent to avoid prolonged stress" (p. 128). It also seems prudent for companies to consider that increased stress on employees may impair their mental abilities not only in the long run, but also in the short run, which could adversely affect productivity.

The connection between the work environment and medical claims was dramatically demonstrated recently in a study by Stanley J. Bigos. He found that the most common factor among employees who file back injury claims was not job requirements (e.g., heavy lifting), not the individual's strength or flexibility, but job satisfaction. Not only were workers who did not enjoy their jobs 2.5 times more likely to file back injury claims than those who did, but workers who reported high emotional stress were more than twice as likely to file a claim (Port 1991).

Lawsuits

The most extreme consequence of job-related stress is death. Lawsuits charging employers with the death of an employee due to overwork and stress have been increasing in Japan. Families have charged companies with working their loved ones to death. The government of Japan actually has committed $2 million to study the problem of death from overwork, or *karoshi* (Naisbitt 1990). In this country, the workers' compensation system has been used by surviving family members who allege that job pressures and stress have caused suicides. Many of these cases have been settled in favor of the family.

In wrongful discharge suits, companies have been advised to think twice about fighting the charge if punitive damages are a possibility. Punitive damages are frequently disproportionate to the injury suffered by the discharged employee, but they frequently are awarded when the company's actions toward the employee bordered on abuse. Questions to ask when assessing whether a company is liable for punitive damages are: Did the company's actions toward the employee extend beyond normal limits? Did they go beyond the merely unpleasant—were they nasty or even cruel?

If the answers are yes, chances are good that the company will be hit with punitive damages (Fritz 1990). This indicates that judges and juries operate within a value system that considers employee abuse to be unconscionable.

INDIRECT COSTS

Quality

Abusive behavior in the workplace creates fear and mistrust, resentment, hostility, feelings of humiliation, withdrawal, play-it-safe strategies, and hiding mistakes. Quality depends on employee involvement, empowerment, trust; fixing the problem rather than fixing blame; dedication to delighting the customer; reliance on data; being a learning organization; and using mistakes as improvement opportunities. An abusive environment clearly is the antithesis of what is needed to support quality efforts in organizations.

W. Edwards Deming (1982), who started the quality movement, says that quality is impossible where people are afraid to tell the truth. Fear causes less-than-full participation in the organization. In order for quality to exist, people must be fully engaged in the organization. Effective problem solving is contingent upon using valid data, and the data will not be valid unless people are willing to tell the truth. If they are afraid of being punished, if they perceive a shoot-the-messenger mentality in the organization, no one will be willing to be frank. People may not actually give false information to the data collection effort of a quality improvement process, but they may not tell the full truth. Important data can be obscured easily by such a play-it-safe strategy. Fear therefore can cripple the simplest attempts to gather data and use it to solve business problems.

Abusive treatment also causes people to be less than fully engaged in the organization. Abused employees have a primary goal, which is to protect themselves. They are therefore unable to fully participate and engage themselves in the organization. To be fully engaged requires suspending one's own self-interest, at least temporarily, and identifying with the larger organization. Employees who have been abused will be reluctant to suspend their own self-interest. They hold back in order to protect themselves, and this holding back is not necessarily a conscious decision, although it is a perfectly natural one.

What this means is that even if management believes that employees' fear and mistrust are misperceptions, it must treat their effects as real. Even if the employees are off-base, the fear and mistrust they feel are real and affect their behavior. It is necessary to get to the bottom of why these misperceptions are endemic in the organization. Until that is done effectively, and until management designs some effective strategies to turn around the cycle of mistrust, efforts to embed quality are doomed. Managers cannot ignore the "messy stuff" of people's feelings and concentrate only on the rational strategy of implementing total quality throughout the organization. It will fail.

High Turnover

The NWNL study cites increased turnover as one of the effects of high-stress at work. Although only 14 percent of employees said that workplace stress caused them to quit or change jobs within the previous two years, more than one-third of new employees said that they left their previous job because of stress (Walters 1991). Wilson (1991) cites high turnover in a department as one indication of an abusive manager there. When an employee's boss is abusive, the employee may have no effective means of ameliorating the situation short of leaving.

Absenteeism

Abused employees frequently will show increased absenteeism. Wilson (1991) lists absenteeism or coming late to work as one sign of workplace trauma. One of the managers interviewed by Toffler (1986) described a situation in which an employee, suffering harassment from her boss, used the excuse of jury duty as a way to get away from the office and her boss. She was actually on jury duty for two days, but she changed the form so that it read twelve days. Since this person was an excellent employee, it was not immediately obvious why she would do such a thing. Upon investigation, the human resource manager discovered that this employee's boss harassed her on the job. One example was that he ridiculed her for going to jury duty because she could not speak English well. There were other problems with the manager, including his sexual harassment of female employees. The employee simply could not face coming to work and found a way to get a respite. The price she paid was the loss of her job.

Another example is offered by Voluck and Abramson (1987). An employee experienced continual supervisory criticism of his work in the presence of others. He developed a fear of going to work; he began to come in late and resorted to taking vacation days to avoid work. The abusive work situation created enormous stress for the employee, resulting in compensable mental injury as judged by the court.

In addition to fear and anxiety, stress and abuse can cause a variety of physical illnesses. It has been estimated that employees who suffer from stress-related illnesses lose an average of sixteen days of work per year as a result (Allen 1990).

Poor Customer Relationships

Employees' view of their employer is heavily influenced by their relationship with their own manager. Employees who feel abused by their manager will be more likely to have a poor perception of their company, and this will come through in their dealings with customers. Not only will they be less likely to go the extra mile for the customer, feeling cheated themselves, but they also are more likely to be abusive to customers.

A company in the service sector had several service centers in which employees handled customer complaints over the phone. The company had decided to consolidate some of these service centers, and one office was going to close down entirely, leaving employees with the choice of taking a transfer or not having a job. If they transferred, it was very likely that they would have to relocate. Employees were so disgruntled that when customers called, they were greeted with obscene remarks. When employees feel abused, they do not care enough or have the energy to go the extra mile for the customer and they might also get a perverse satisfaction out of harming their employer by treating customers badly, even though this harms them as well.

Sabotage and Revenge

Winokur (1990) gives several instances of vengeful acts against companies or bosses by employees who perceive they are being wronged by their employers. The perception of injustice stems mainly from the almost steady downsizing of the 1980s. One employee was found in a company parking lot, lying in wait for his supervisor with a loaded gun. Another retaliated in a very risky way against a boss who passed her over for a deserved promotion. Knowing that her boss's productivity was being scrutinized, she began to subtly make mistakes and delay project completions. When her boss wrote a negative job evaluation that he placed in her employment file without talking to her about it first, she wrote a lengthy memo disputing the evaluation and sent copies to her boss's superiors. This badly hurt her boss's credibility; he was fired within a few months and she got his job. In yet another incident, an employee almost ruined the firm that employed her by planting rumors with the local media about alleged financial improprieties by her boss. The firm lost a number of its clients, and by the time the newspapers printed retractions, her boss had spent $30,000 in tax attorney's fees to clear her name.

Acts of sabotage by laid-off employees are common, especially the destruction of records and computer data. Human resource executives at large companies are aware of destructive outbursts by laid-off managers. Although they do not discuss them publicly, they admit privately that these incidents happen (Smith 1988). Given the ubiquity of computer systems, a disgruntled employee could sabotage an entire system and cause massive confusion and lost productivity.

People turn to revenge when they believe that they have been slighted and feel the need to repair the damage done to them, says Ronald S. Ebert of the Levinson Institute (Winokur 1990). While an objective observer might consider the slight to be minor, to the individual who feels harmed, it is significant. It is the perception of injustice that counts and that causes the employee to take action, whether that action be an act of revenge or sabotage, or, in other cases, litigation (Wilson 1991).

OPPORTUNITY COSTS

Opportunity costs are the least visible of the three categories of costs discussed in this chapter. These costs are not really costs per se; the term refers to what is lost by not pursuing an activity or strategy that could bring in revenue. Entrepreneurs, self-employed people, and consultants are quite familiar with this concept. They must estimate their opportunity costs and make cost/benefit decisions whenever they put in considerable time on any one project. When a consultant signs a contract to work with a client on retainer, he or she is giving up other opportunities for the sake of working with that client. The consultant must ensure his or her own financial viability and must therefore make sure that the work to be undertaken is worth it. In other words, the contracted work must be at least equivalent to the value of the lost opportunities. In determining the fee for the work, opportunity costs must be factored in.

This concept can be applied to organizational functioning and particularly to company policies and practices regarding employees. What are the opportunity costs associated with adopting a particular policy? With having certain beliefs about employees' values? With particular management practices? For instance, what might be the opportunity costs associated with electronically monitoring employee telephone conversations with customers? In order to determine what those opportunity costs are, one would have to identify what behavior ideally is desired in the customer contact situation, discover what the impact of the monitoring is on employee behavior, and consider how behavior might be affected under different conditions (e.g., with a different policy, with group monitoring and group problem solving when needed, by abandoning time requirements for individual calls and focusing instead on customer satisfaction, etc.).

There are opportunity costs associated with employee abuse and with the organization tolerating and rewarding managers who practice it. In order to conceptualize what those opportunity costs might be, it is necessary to construct a mental image of an environment totally opposite to one characterized by employee abuse. An abusive environment results in fear, mistrust, resentment, hostility, feelings of humiliation, a sense of powerlessness and of being devalued, withdrawal, playing it safe, hiding mistakes (and therefore not learning from those mistakes), and so on. The antithesis of this environment would be one in which employees feel trusted, valued, empowered, confident, involved, supported, willing to try new behavior and learn from mistakes, committed to delighting the customer, confident that mistakes will be viewed by others as learning opportunities, and much more. The opportunity cost is whatever the organization misses by not having the second kind of environment.

In this environment, employees would be committed, putting forth their maximum effort to help the organization be successful, exercising their creativity, getting satisfaction from delighting customers. In some of these environments, employees have been observed running from their cars to their offices in the morning.

Environments that stamp out this kind of commitment suffer enormous opportunity costs, although they usually don't realize it. The attitudes and beliefs of senior managers prevent them from trusting employees enough to empower them. Abused employees minimize their commitment to their boss, which means that they usually minimize their commitment to their jobs and to their organization's success as well. Some of the effects of that lowered commitment are described below.

Lack of Discretionary Effort

Discretionary effort is the difference between the maximum effort of which one is capable and the minimum effort one must give in order to avoid being fired (Bean 1989). Everyone has a choice about how much effort to give every day. Federal Express is one company that has worked to create an environment in which employees will choose to exert maximum discretionary effort. In order to do this, it did not simply exhort employees to work harder, as many companies have chosen to do. Instead, it believes that employees need five things in order to perform: clarity of expectations, encouragement, justice, job security, and rewards. It works to create an environment that encourages risk taking, tolerates failure, gives employees a voice by reviewing supervisor performance, educates every employee on the company's values and strategies, enables supervisors to reward performance spontaneously and creatively, supports a grievance procedure that ensures being heard, and eschews layoffs. An empowering environment in this company creates empowered employees and peak performance.

Jan Carlzon gives a wonderful example of discretionary effort in his 1987 book about the transformation of Scandinavian Airlines (SAS). A customer arrived at the airport and realized that he had left his ticket in his room at the hotel. Instead of preventing the customer from boarding the flight until he could produce the ticket, or until some bureaucratic procedures were gone through to get a new one, the SAS agent gave the customer a temporary ticket, called his hotel, sent an SAS limousine to the hotel where the hotel staff retrieved the ticket from the customer's room, and handed the customer's ticket to him before his flight took off. The customer was surprised and delighted with the excellent service. He most likely told dozens of people about this experience, which enhanced the reputation of SAS and probably won it future business.

An employee who feels abused, on the other hand, will most likely not exercise discretionary effort. If the abuse is severe or long-lasting enough, the employee may give only the minimum effort required to avoid losing his or her job. Many abused employees are punished by their bosses no matter what they do, so they learn to invest the minimum, since the result will be the same anyway. Other abused employees may feel such anger and resentment that they are unwilling to invest more of themselves than absolutely necessary.

There are tremendous opportunity costs when a talented person does not exercise discretionary effort in their job. Productivity suffers, customer satisfaction may suffer, there may be unquantifiable differences in revenues, opportunities for process improvement may slip by . . . and the list goes on. The difference between discretionary effort and minimum acceptable effort may be the difference between a delighted customer and one who is merely satisfied. More and more companies are coming to the realization that merely satisfying customers is not enough; in order to be perceived as the best, it is necessary to strive to delight customers. The difference between giving a minimum acceptable performance and a maximum discretionary effort in order to delight the customer is the opportunity cost.

Discretionary effort cannot be forced or coerced. It is a gift that can only be given freely. It can be enabled by enlightened managers who value their people and effectively communicate that they value them. Abusive managers will never get discretionary effort from the employees they abuse. Managers who create an empowering environment will receive not only discretionary effort but also levels of performance consistently beyond their expectations. When employees feel that it is worth their while to invest themselves, they exercise discretionary effort, and the organization reaps the reward.

Many managers appear to think that employees owe their bosses and their companies discretionary effort. They judge harshly any employee who does not exert it. This is just another form of abuse. It is a manager's responsibility to create the environment that will elicit discretionary effort from employees, not to blame employees if they choose not to exercise it. Employees don't owe their managers discretionary effort any more than they owe them respect—both must be earned. How do managers know when they have created the appropriate environment? They see discretionary effort. It will never fail to appear, because people do what they are rewarded for.

Commitments Outside the Job

Employees who are abused tend to disengage from their workplace. In order to keep a positive focus in their lives, they often find activities outside of work that will grow in importance in their lives. In fact, the healthier the employee is, the more likely he or she will find other commitments outside of work in which to get involved.

Such disengagement from work and re-engagement in outside activities is a healthy response to a dysfunctional work situation. Employees who don't do this will find themselves caught in a negative spiral. Work has become unpleasant, and if they continue to have their work be of prime importance in their lives, then they are choosing to value a negative emotional experience, which feels terrible. Unless the employee can turn around the situation at work, which is rarely the case, there is only one way to get positive emotional experiences: get them somewhere else. Most people are not masochists and will do exactly that.

This behavior has become so commonplace that the *Wall Street Journal* ran an article on what it called "defensive entrepreneurs" (Mitchell 1990). It included profiles of three employees who had started businesses on their own in order to generate their own individual sense of employment security, knowing that they could not depend on their companies for continued employment. Each of them had started their businesses as a moonlighting venture, while they were still employed. Two of them had since left their jobs, taking advantage of early retirement offers to devote themselves full-time to their businesses.

This brings up another practical consideration. There are only so many hours in a day. When employees devote significant amounts of energy to moonlighting on second jobs, building their own businesses, and so forth, they of necessity put less energy into their full-time jobs with their primary employer. One manager in a large company said, "Everyone in this office has a second job. Some of them are starting their own businesses, some are preparing for a second career by attending school, others are simply working the late shift somewhere else. They keep this job for the benefits. But they are refusing to travel on business anymore, because they have this other business. They're not staying late, they're not working overtime, they're not investing themselves in order to help the company succeed. They're looking out for themselves because they know the company doesn't care about them."

These employees are just putting in time. Their insecurity, although it may not result from a situation of actual abuse, drives them to build other sources of security in their lives. Abused employees find it necessary to disengage in the same ways, and for some of the same reasons. An employee who is abused by the boss fears that he or she may lose their job at any time and will also be driven to disengage from the work situation and pour energy into other activities, not only to provide some kind of safety net for the future but also to maintain a sense of self-esteem and enjoyment in life.

The organization loses in all of these situations. Large numbers of employees are not exercising discretionary effort because their energies are divided between their primary job and some other activity that is becoming more important to them. The opportunity costs of employees developing other kinds of work commitments are huge. It is not just time that is being denied to the primary job, it is also mental energy. If an employee finds it necessary to invest in some other activity to gain self-esteem because the boss makes his or her life miserable, that other activity will assume primary importance in the employee's life psychologically. He or she will go above and beyond the call of duty for the alternative interest but will be unlikely to do so for the abusive boss. A company that tolerates abusive management will find it very difficult to achieve its organizational goals of total quality and employee involvement, because these depend upon employee commitment.

Time Spent Talking about the Problem

Employees of an abusive boss spend significant amounts of time discussing the situation and helping each other survive. They share insights, strategies, and approaches to managing the boss. They fantasize about a better situation, they keep each other posted on the latest rumors, and they share can-you-top-this stories. These are all survival strategies that enable them to maintain their mental health as best they can. But all of the time that they put into propping up their own and their peers' spirits is time that is not spent on the work for which the company is paying them. If they didn't have to put so much effort into staying sane, they could put that effort into their work. Again, the company loses a large amount of discretionary effort.

Loss of Creativity

Employee abuse creates fear and anxiety, which are incompatible with creativity. The same stressful conditions that have led to an increase in employee abuse also serve to stifle creativity. Certain conditions are necessary for creativity to flourish, one of which is the time to play with ideas while in an open mode of thinking: relaxed, expansive, less purposeful, more contemplative (Cleese 1991). Organizationally, this translates into administrative slack. Peter Drucker relates a company's ability to innovate to the amount of administrative slack it provides in its daily operations ("Creativity in Danger" 1991). With downsizing's focus on cutting out fat, cutting costs, doing more with less, and so forth, there is far too little administrative slack in today's organizations.

The key to increasing creativity is not to focus on the individual level, but to build an organizational climate in which creativity can flourish ("More on Fostering Creativity" 1991). One of the primary characteristics of such an environment is trust so that people can try out new ideas and fail without fearing punishment. Trust is sorely lacking when employees are abused. As Cleese (1991) says, "If there's one person around who makes you feel defensive, you'll lose the confidence to play, and it's goodbye creativity," (p. 15). If employees do not trust their boss to support them, if they are continually feeling threatened and in fear of punishment and reprisal, there can be no creativity.

Quality and continuous improvement depend on people's creative and innovative ideas. It follows that where there is employee abuse, attempts to embed continuous improvement in an organization's operations will be hampered. The fear that exists in such organizations prevents creative and innovative solutions from being generated. The organization can never reach its potential, which exemplifies this kind of opportunity cost.

SUMMARY

It should be clear that organizations make unmeasurable sacrifices in productivity and profitability by tolerating employee abuse. What makes the losses unmeasurable is the concept of opportunity costs. One cannot measure something that isn't there; no one knows how productive a person can be under different circumstances. As Ryan and Oestreich (1991) point out, in organizations where fear is prevalent, the organization generally will survive and may even be reasonably successful. The important question is, how much more successful could it be? No one can say, because lost opportunities cannot be measured, especially if their possible existence is not even considered.

In order to even conceptualize the opportunity costs involved with employee abuse, it is necessary to envision a different environment. The companies that are able to do this will have a much better chance of eliminating employee abuse.

REFERENCES

Allen, D. S. 1990. Less stress, less litigation. *Personnel* (January): 32–35.

Bean, F. T. 1989. Employee empowerment at Federal Express. Talk given at Human Resource Institute Issue Management Conference, St. Petersburg, Fla., February 8–10.

Buderi, R. 1991. Developments to watch: The rat race is rough—ask any rat. *Business Week* (May 20): 128.

Carlzon, J. 1987. *Moments of truth.* Cambridge, Mass.: Ballinger.

Cleese, J. 1991. And now for something completely different. *Personnel: AMA's HR Focus* (April): 13–15.

Creativity in danger: Causes and cures. 1991. *Human Resource Management News* (January 5): 4.

Deming, W. E. 1982. *Out of the crisis.* Cambridge, Mass.: Massachusetts Institute of Technology, Center for Advanced Engineering Study.

Fritz, N. R. 1990. HR Focus: Profits before pride. *Personnel* (April): 4.

Klaft, R. P. and Kleiner, B. H. 1988. Understanding workaholics. *Business* (July-September): 37–40.

LaVan, H.; Katz, M.; and Hochwarter, W. 1990. Employee stress swamps workers' comp. *Personnel* (May): 61–64.

Mitchell, J. 1990. Eye on the future: Fear of layoff spurs employees to launch part-time businesses. *Wall Street Journal* (May 25): A1.

More on fostering creativity. 1991. *Human Resource Management News* (July 8): 2.

Naisbitt, J. 1990. In Japan, take time off or else . . . . *John Naisbitt's Trend Letter* (October 25): 8.

Pasternak, C. 1991a. HRM update: Costly job stress. *HR Magazine* (September): 24.

———. 1991b. HRM update: Depression no. 1. *HR Magazine* (October): 22.

Poe, R. and Baker, E. L. 1990. Stress is taking its toll in the American workplace. *Across the Board* (May): 8.

Port, O., ed. 1991. Developments to watch. *Business Week* (April 1): 82.

Ryan, K. D. and Oestreich, D. K. 1991. *Driving fear out of the workplace.* San Francisco: Jossey-Bass.

Scott, J. 1991. New study links stress to catching a cold. *San Francisco Chronicle* (August 29): A1.

Scovel, K. 1991. Personnel update: Stressed out. *Human Resource Executive* (July): 14.

Smith, E. T. 1988. Stress: The test Americans are failing. *Business Week* (April 18): 74–76.

This week's news at a glance. 1990. *Human Resource Management News* (May 5): 1.

Toffler, B. L. 1986. *Tough choices: Managers talk ethics.* New York: John Wiley & Sons.

Voluck, P. R. and Abramson, H. 1987. How to avoid stress-related disability claims. *Personnel Journal* (May): 95–98.

Walters, R. W. and Associates, eds. 1991. Is job stress too high? *Behavioral Sciences Newsletter* (October 14): 3–4.

Wilson, C. B. 1991. U.S. businesses suffer from workplace trauma. *Personnel Journal* (July): 47–50.

Winokur, L. A. 1990. Sweet revenge is souring the office. *Wall Street Journal* (September 19): B1.

11

Corporate Response to Employee Abuse

This chapter will examine what corporations have done to address employee abuse. Programs and interventions discussed will of necessity be less than comprehensive, since no company to my knowledge has identified the entire problem as yet, although some are beginning to come to grips with the issues involved. Many of the programs to be discussed focus on helping individual employees cope with stress and problems at work. Until these programs bring in a more organizational focus, the issues involved with employee abuse will not be successfully addressed.

CORPORATE OMBUDSMEN AND ETHICS OFFICES

With the rising concern about business ethics in corporate America, many companies have established an ombudsman, ethical ombudsman, or ethics office responsible for bringing employees' ethical concerns to the attention of top management. Although the most frequent cases dealt with by these offices have to do with how employees are treated by their managers, that is not generally why the offices were created. Literature about ombudsmen is scanty, but among the recent writings the following reasons have been proposed for establishing an ombudsman function: to reverse the public's negative perception of business (Futter 1990), to deal with bad news internally in order to avoid public scandals (Brody 1986), to influence ethical behavior among employees (McDonald and Zepp 1990), and to bring employee concerns to the attention of top management (Scherba 1986; McClelland 1988). In 1986, 8 percent of Fortune 500 companies had established an ethical ombudsman ("Are Corporations Institutionalizing Ethics?" 1986). In 1991, more than 15 percent of companies employing fifty thousand or more people had ethics offices, most of which had been created within the previous five years (Feder 1991).

Probably one of the more fascinating findings about ethics and ombudsmens' offices is that the largest percentage of calls involve personnel issues: fair treatment by supervisors, promotions, performance evaluations, boss/subordinate conflicts, and so forth. NYNEX, whose ethics office was established in 1990, found that 42 percent of its calls were about personnel matters (Feder 1991). Other companies whose offices have been in operation longer have experienced the same pattern, and sometimes the percentage is quite a bit higher. Some companies, like General Dynamics, have accepted this unexpected finding and presumably used it for organizational learning. "One lesson that is hard to learn is that the primary way most employees measure corporate ethics is whether they are fairly treated," says General Dynamics's vice-president in charge of ethics (Feder 1991). Other companies choose to ignore the significance of such findings and direct personnel calls to the human resources department. When a company misinterprets the fact that large numbers of employees view how they are treated as an ethical issue and labels their concerns as belonging in the human resources arena, the probability is very low that employee abuse will be identified as a legitimate problem that needs corporate attention.

Although ethics offices and corporate ombudsman functions were not usually created in response to the problem of employee abuse, they are yielding important data about the extent and severity of the problem. Companies that have such offices would be wise to monitor the frequency of calls having to do with employee treatment and employee/supervisory relations. Depending on the frequency of the calls and the types of problems uncovered, there may be a need to approach the issue on an organizational level rather than on an individual basis.

EMPLOYEE ASSISTANCE PROGRAMS

An ongoing concern for productivity is responsible for the growth of employee assistance programs (EAPs) in this country. EAPs originally were designed to help employees who had alcohol problems. They gradually expanded their focus and now refer employees with a variety of problems to appropriate professional help. In recent years, substance abuse and stress management have been major issues for most EAPs. They are designed to identify troubled employees and make referrals for assistance before disciplinary action becomes an issue. Improved productivity and lower health insurance premiums are advantages of a well-run EAP (Neddermeyer 1986).

EAPs are generally not set up to identify organizational problems. They tend to operate from a medical model that approaches problem behavior from the standpoint of individual dysfunction. However, the way that EAPs are used has been changing. In the beginning, employees were referred to an EAP because of a drinking problem. Occasionally employees would voluntarily seek the help of the EAP, but generally the denial mechanisms of alcoholics prevented them from seeking help before a decrement in performance was noted by others. Performance was the key reason for referring an employee to an EAP, and still is. However, EAPs are no longer associated as strongly with treatment for alcoholism. Many work in concert with company wellness programs and offer assistance with various kinds of problems in living. Employees now seek the help of EAPs not only for substance abuse problems but for family relationship problems, work/family conflicts, stress reduction, and conflicts at work.

Although EAPs, like ethics offices, were not designed to address the problems of employee abuse in the workplace, they can be a valuable source of data regarding the state of the boss/subordinate relationship in general. Although the nature of individual EAP contacts must remain confidential, it is feasible to track summary data regarding categories of problems. The nature of contacts with EAP counselors can be tracked over time and correlated with major organizational events such as downsizings, reorganizations, cost-cutting initiatives, budget pressures, changes in corporate policies, and the like. A company concerned about the problem of employee abuse could use such data to track organizational health and the prevalence of dysfunctional supervisory conduct.

WELLNESS PROGRAMS

Rising medical costs have spurred many companies to invest in company wellness programs. These programs are designed to give employees information and support about lifestyle choices that can improve their health and well-being. Programs adopt a preventive approach and encourage good diet, exercise, weight loss, smoking cessation, prenatal care, and so forth.

Many programs offer stress management classes to employees. Although this was not the primary reason wellness programs came into existence, they are serving a growing need for employees who find themselves under increasing amounts of stress. Abused employees may find some relief from the negative effects of having an abusive manager by learning better techniques of managing their personal response to stress. However, stress management in such a situation offers merely symptomatic relief. The wellness program is limited in the kind of help it can provide for employees who find themselves stuck in a relationship with a dysfunctional boss.

This in fact, is the general limitation with wellness programs. They approach health on an individual level, and it is a rare wellness program that has an organizational focus. This limitation frequently frustrates those in charge of such programs. They realize that many of the health-related issues with which employees struggle go beyond personal lifestyle choices to a dysfunctional organizational system, yet they lack the power to do anything about the larger organizational issues.

In the future wellness programs may well become more comprehensive to include an organizational component. In the meantime, senior management is advised to listen to the perspective of the people who run their wellness programs, with regard to organizational issues that affect employee health and well-being. Not doing so could mean significant opportunity costs for the organization.

NONUNION GRIEVANCE SYSTEMS

Labor unions have been instrumental in establishing grievance procedures for represented employees. Employees regard this service as one of the most important functions of a labor union (Bohlander and White 1988). Nonrepresented employees, however, usually have no established procedures that they can use to express dissatisfactions and problems with unfair treatment. Many companies have sought to address this vacuum by creating a nonunion grievance system. One such system, Federal Express's Guaranteed Fair Treatment Procedure, was discussed in Chapter 5.

Bohlander and White (1988) reported on a study of grievance procedures in nonunion, private-sector organizations. Since the analysis was done only on companies that are not unionized, very little is known about grievance procedures that may exist for nonrepresented employees in unionized companies. Several important findings emerged from this survey. The first is that the implementation of these programs is a very recent development. The great majority had been implemented since 1980 and many since 1986. Reasons for implementing grievance systems also were assessed, both formally (as part of the policy statement) and informally (through interviews). Reasons given in policy or philosophy statements included: to foster good communication between employees and their supervisors, to build a foundation for a healthy work relationship, to ensure that employee problems are recognized and appropriately reviewed, to maintain a friendly atmosphere in which employees can have a rewarding work experience, and to serve as a recourse when employees believe they have not been treated in accordance with company policies. In interviews, company human resource managers mentioned several other reasons for implementing a grievance system. These included: to place a check on supervisors' interpretation and implementation of management decisions, to encourage higher productivity, to reduce turnover, to prevent union organization, and to avoid costly and embarrassing litigation.

Do these grievance mechanisms accomplish what they intend to? Implementing the grievance system is a good start; however, that alone does not ensure that employees truly have recourse for unfair treatment. Many employers are aware that a significant barrier to the success of a grievance system is fear—employees' fear that they will be retaliated against if they use the system to attempt to redress a wrong. Most of the responding organizations in the previously mentioned study attempted to address this concern by guaranteeing in their policy statements that employees can bring problems to the attention of management without fear of reprisal. One policy clearly stated that no employee may be "harassed, intimidated, discharged, or otherwise disciplined" for using the process or participating in it.

Unfortunately, such guarantees in written policy statements suffer from the same credibility problem that the existence of the grievance system itself does. No one can guarantee that a manager will not retaliate in any way. As we have seen in prior chapters of this book, some forms of employee abuse can be very subtle. A clever manager wishing to get back at a subordinate for airing a grievance and causing embarrassment can manage to do so without it seeming to be in direct retaliation. Bohlander and White (1988) point out that most employees in their study did believe that supervisors would hold it against them if they were to use the grievance procedure. They point out that having a potentially effective and fair grievance procedure is not enough to ensure its success, but that management must make special efforts to use it correctly. However, given all the advantages and potential disadvantages, it is probably still better to have a grievance procedure than not to have one. The biggest mistake of all would be to institute a grievance procedure while making no effort to change the corporate culture in ways that can enhance its success.

EMPLOYEE SURVEYS

In some companies, surveys are done regularly in order to gauge employee opinion and morale. Usually it is possible to obtain data for different departments as well as companywide data, and some companies provide data down to the level of individual manager. IBM uses survey data provided by a manager's subordinates to help the manager improve his or her managerial skill. In IBM's system, subordinates are seen as an important source of data about a manager's ability to coach, develop, and support subordinates. In order for such a practice to work well, it must be integrated into the company's culture in a way that facilitates trust.

Other companies don't have corporate cultures that can support the use of survey data in such a direct way. Even in these companies, however, summary data about abusive management practices could still be quite useful for an organization wanting to understand more about the problems of treating employees fairly. Specifically worded questions can tap information about the extent and severity of employee abuse in the company. Open-ended questions can elicit more detailed accounts of the employees' perspective of such situations.

SUMMARY

Since the problem of abusive management has only begun to surface in organizations, there has been very little corporate response to date. Nevertheless, this review has shown that there is significant potential in programs that already exist. Companies that are fortunate enough to have several of the programs discussed in this chapter can use them to gather data on the extent of the problem and can use the information to develop an integrated approach to the issues.

Corporate Ombudsmen and Ethics Offices

Instead of redirecting calls about personnel issues to the human resource department, companies are urged to use their ombudsman or ethics office staff to track the nature of abusive treatment of employees by supervisors and managers. Each individual call should, of course, be handled according to the procedures developed by the office that receives it. Data from those calls can be categorized and summarized in order to shed light on what is happening in the organization. Collected in this way, the data will protect the confidentiality of the callers while still providing necessary information on the nature and frequency of abusive management practices.

Employee Assistance Programs

Data on the specific types of problems for which employees seek help are probably already being collected in employee assistance programs. With some slight modifications, the existing data collection procedures will be sufficient to provide the information necessary for the organization to learn more about the problem of employee abuse. Employee assistance counselors would need some training in the problem of employee abuse in order to be able to spot possible cases. If an employee is directly seeking help for a problem with his or her boss, the counselor will need to gather some additional detail about the situation before referring the employee to outside help, if it is warranted. The additional data would not be collected with the intention of assessing relative guilt or innocence but in order to understand more about the specific behaviors demonstrated by both the manager and the subordinate.

Wellness Programs

These programs are not necessarily set up to gather data about individual management relationships. However, there may be trend data regarding problematical mental and physical symptoms available from various programs within the wellness framework. Those involved in the wellness program have a unique organizational perspective, and their insights on health trends can provide useful information about organizational dynamics. The company's wellness program can be tapped in imaginative ways in order to provide additional information regarding abusive management practices and corporate culture.

Nonunion Grievance Systems

Extremely useful information may be obtained from grievance procedures with some additional effort by those involved. Bohlander and White (1988) report that few organizations keep formal records of the number, type, or ultimate resolution of grievances, and that most organizations that do keep records have very few cases that proceed to the formal grievance stage. That is because most employee grievances (approximately 80 percent) are resolved at informal initial meetings between the grievant and his or her immediate supervisor. Since those meetings are not considered part of the formal grievance process, they are not officially recorded.

Still, some information must be available in order for human resource managers to report that 80 percent get resolved before formal grievance procedures take effect. In fact, the operating philosophy of many of these systems is to attempt to resolve the grievances at the lowest possible level. The issue may be one of recording some very basic information at the time the initial inquiry or grievance is filed. Items such as job title or function of the complainant, nature of the problem, relationship of the complainant to the person about which the complaint is being made, policy issue or employee rights alleged to have been violated, specific behavior objected to, and other information can be collected and summarized. Follow-up procedures can then record how and at what level the problem was resolved.

Employee Surveys

A wealth of information can be obtained from employee surveys regarding supervisory relationships within the company. General questions usually are asked about the degree of support employees get from their managers, how effectively performance appraisals are done, and so forth. Adding some focused questions about specific supervisory behavior in different situations, as well as how this behavior affects employees, can yield information about abusive practices.

Senior management may be reluctant to open the door to these kinds of issues, fearing it would create more problems than it would solve, and employees might be encouraged to view situations in a more negative light than they might otherwise. Nothing could be further from the truth. If the corporate culture tolerates abusive conduct by managers, the organization is already experiencing negative effects. Not acknowledging it will not make it go away. Acknowledging the possibility will not create an issue out of a nonissue.

What about the objection that, if abuse was a problem, then employees would have brought it to higher management on their own? That may be true with other problems, but not with employee abuse. Chapter 3's discussion on power in organizations explains why employees are unlikely to create waves when they are experiencing abuse from bosses. Not talking about it does not mean that there is no problem; the nature of the hierarchy prevents the problem from being raised at higher levels. Employees may not be telling higher management about the problem, but if it exists, it is guaranteed to affect the profitability of the company.

On the other hand, if employees feel supported and encouraged by their managers, they will answer survey questions about their managers positively. Adding a few questions to a survey that tap the nature and extent of abusive practices will not influence employees to answer negatively.

Survey questions and responses cannot create a problem where none exists already; all they can do is clarify the nature of an existing problem or yield reassurances that the problem does not exist.

What Next?

Information gathered from all of the above sources can be used to audit the company culture. Questions like "To what extent do we live out our belief that people are our most important resource?" and "How are we succeeding at driving fear out of the organization?" can be answered by examining what the data say about the health of supervisory relationships in the company. One caution, however: negative data say something significant about the level of fear and blame in the culture. In this sort of culture, there will be a great temptation to go on a witch hunt. It is of crucial importance to not do this. Not only will it not solve the problem, it will just reinforce—and justify—the fear in the culture. This approach would also be useless because the problem is not that there are some abusive managers who need to be fired; the problem is that the culture supports and rewards abusive management. Remove the most abusive managers, and they will be replaced by others who will match them in abusiveness. This strategy can only identify scapegoats while ignoring the values in the culture that encourage and reward abusive behavior.

It is advisable to follow W. Edwards Deming's (1982) advice on using data for continuous improvement. Reasons for negative data need to be explored. As Deming says, "Good leadership requires investigation into possible causes." The causes are always in the system—in this case the corporate culture. In order to change the corporate culture, senior management must rigorously and honestly assess its own personal value system and examine what kind of role model it needs to be to accomplish the needed changes. This will not be easy, nor will it be quick. Feedback mechanisms will need to be established to assess how well senior management is demonstrating new behavior. When the inevitable regressions to old behavior occur, they can be corrected. This discussion is not to imply that senior managers are to blame for an abusive culture. They may not have created it, but they did succeed in it, and they therefore are the only ones who can be the role models of the new, more desirable culture.

REFERENCES

Are corporations institutionalizing ethics? 1986. *Journal of Business Ethics* (Netherlands) (April): 85–91.

Bohlander, G. W. and White, H. C. 1988. Building bridges? Nonunion employee grievance systems. *Personnel* (July): 62–66.

Brody, M. 1986. Listen to your whistleblower. *Fortune* (November 24): 77–78.

Deming, W. E. 1982. *Out of the crisis*. Cambridge, Mass.: Massachusetts Institute of Technology Center for Advanced Engineering Study.

Feder, B. J. 1991. Helping corporate America hew to the straight and narrow. *New York Times* (November 3): F5.

Futter, V. 1990. An answer to the public perception of corporations: A corporate ombudsperson? *Business Lawyer* (November): 29–56.

McClelland, V. A. 1988. Upward communication: Is anyone listening? *Personnel Journal* (June): 124–31.

McDonald, G. M. and Zepp, R. A. 1990. What should be done? A practical approach to business ethics. *Management Decision* (UK) 28 (1): 9–14.

Neddermeyer, D. M. 1986. Employee assistance programs: Tackling emotional dysfunctioning in the workplace. *Nonprofit World* (September-October): 24–27.

Scherba, J. 1986. Improving personnel performance with an employee ombudsman. *Bank Administration* (November): 66–68.

Part IV
Solutions

The first two chapters in this last section focus on what companies need to do to address the problem of employee abuse. Solutions are recommended in the context of an organization development effort that focuses on cultural change. Efforts such as increasing quality, managing and valuing diversity, and addressing work/family balance issues are explored for their potential to eliminate employee abuse.

A model is proposed that can be used by senior management to assess the corporate culture with regard to employee abuse. The model enables leaders to examine the values and belief systems that support organizational policies, practices, and reward systems. Leaders will also be able to look at whether values and behavior in the organization are consistent, and whether publicly stated values match the value system that can be inferred from the everyday behavior of managers in the organization. Feedback is emphasized as an important component of both cultural assessment and cultural change, as is the necessity of senior management to consciously model behavior consistent with the ideal culture they want to create.

Finally, the last chapter provides a vision of the transformative changes that are occurring in the workplace. These changes are related to new relationships between employers and employees, and between employees and their coaches. Suggestions are given for employers that wish to incorporate the new values about people into their road maps for the future.

12

Guidance for Employers

This chapter develops a framework for senior management to ensure that abusive management is not tolerated. Unfortunately, this is not a simple or easy task. It cannot be accomplished merely by a statement of values or mission. They certainly will not hurt, but they are not sufficient to ensure that employee abuse does not occur in the organization.

Senior management sets the tone for the culture in the organization. If employee abuse is a problem, something in the environment is supporting it. By looking at the situation in this way, senior management can use the problem as an opportunity to fine-tune the organizational culture. Its efforts can make the company even more successful by making it a better place to work. Senior management needs to determine what aspects of the organizational culture are supporting abusive management practices in order to make appropriate changes.

ROLE OF SENIOR MANAGEMENT

In any effort for change, senior management is the role model for the rest of the organization. Where employee abuse has been identified as a problem, senior management's role model is even more important, because many managers will treat their subordinates as they are treated by their bosses. By observing their manager's behavior, employees learn what it takes to get ahead in the organization. A large part of the manager's visible behavior is his or her behavior toward subordinates. Management style observed at the top of the organization will filter down, with each successive layer of management observing how it is treated by the layer above. If changes are necessary in how managers treat employees, the behavior must be exhibited by those at the top.

Leadership must also communicate a strong sense of values with regard to people and their contributions to the organization. This is not as easy as it sounds. It is not enough for the senior leadership team to say "Our people are our most important resource," or "We value the individual," or even "Everything we do must respect the dignity of the individual." It is also necessary to ensure that other aspects of the culture support those values. These other aspects include organizational policies, management practices, reward systems, training, decision-making processes, budget allocation, and so forth. What the organization does must correspond with what the organization says.

Finally, senior leadership needs to ensure that employees have avenues of recourse to use when they feel they are being treated unfairly. Even in organizations where values about the dignity and worth of people are sincere and deeply believed, and where organizational systems have been designed to support those values, there will be times when it does not work right. People are not infallible. Managers make mistakes, some personality conflicts are unresolvable, people sometimes make hasty decisions under pressure, and the system breaks down. Safety mechanisms must be built in to provide alternative paths for employees to seek justice.

An Organization Development Approach

In order to understand how employee abuse occurs and how to prevent or eliminate it, it is necessary to begin with an understanding of the culture of the organization. This will provide a context and some clues as to what aspects of the organization could contribute to employee abuse or to a hostile work environment. All of the various aspects of the culture of the organization must be evaluated for their potential contribution to the organizational climate. This includes not just statements of values, or how the senior leadership says it would like employees to be treated. It also includes behavior demonstrated by all levels of management in the organization, especially by the senior leadership team, and an honest evaluation of what messages are being communicated by the demonstrated behavior. In other words, senior leaders need feedback on whether their behavior is perceived by managers and employees as being consistent with their stated values. Values, behavior, and feedback are the primary elements in analyzing employee abuse and in changing the organizational climate to eliminate it. Chapter 13 provides more information about this model.

Values. Values are the foundation of organizational culture. Values regarding people, specifically, affect every aspect of organizational behavior. How senior leadership values people influences how employees are treated by the organization and by their management. Although it is sometimes easy to articulate a set of ideal values, and many companies have done so, it is not as easy to ensure that those stated values reflect the true values of the senior leadership team and thus of the organization. If the stated values truly reflect deeply held values of senior leadership, there will likely be congruence among stated values, behavior of managers, policies, and practices with regard to people.

Frequently what leaders say they believe about people is not reflected in their behavior or in the behavior of managers in the organization. Their statements are usually positive about the value of the people in the organization. What is reflected in the organization's behavior may be more negative and pessimistic. This situation may result in employee abuse. Management systems, policies, and practices reflect the true underlying values about people, not necessarily the stated values. Employees are able to see through the stated values and perceive the real values by which the organization operates, resulting in cynicism, a low level of commitment to the organization, and poor morale.

It is more difficult for senior management to perceive those underlying values, recognize them, and own them. No one wants to acknowledge publicly that he or she has a pessimistic view of human nature, does not trust people, or has a generally low opinion of his or her employees. These things may be difficult to admit even to oneself. Nevertheless, as Chapter 4 discusses, American culture in general is deeply entrenched in a model of aversive behavior control (punishment), which predisposes people to concentrate on the negative aspects of others' behavior and results in a Theory X philosophy. We all learn this model, and it affects our beliefs about people as well as our expectations about peoples' behavior. Instilling positive and empowering messages about people requires a conscious effort and a willingness to confront one's own baggage of disempowering beliefs and expectations about people.

Behavior. The behavior of a culture is the set of systems and processes that people can see on a daily basis. The *formal* culture is embodied in policies, procedures, and rules that determine how people are supposed to behave. For instance, managers are required to conduct performance appraisals once a year, employees are rated on managerial potential once a year, available jobs must be advertised internally before an external search begins, data systems are available that contain information on employee training and job experience, employee overtime is to be compensated under certain circumstances. There is also an *informal* culture, which pertains to how things really operate. For instance, although in many organizations performance reviews are required, many managers do not conduct them, and it is possible to find employees who have never had one. Although jobs are supposed to be advertised internally, the internal search often is done merely to satisfy the requirement, with no intention of identifying an internal candidate, because the manager already has a candidate for the job in mind.

At this level of analysis, it is necessary to identify both what the formal and informal cultures say about employee treatment. Discrepancies between the two contain important information. If there is a discrepancy, employees will believe the informal culture. They use the information contained in "how things really operate around here" to infer what the true values are of the organization and of senior leadership. Employees then will act in ways consistent with the values they perceive. If the informal culture says that people are not really valued, managers may infer that abusing subordinates is acceptable. This is why it is so important to get a reading on both the formal and informal cultures and determine the extent of discrepancy between them.

Feedback. An organization is a system of interdependent elements, and feedback is necessary to know how well the system is functioning. Senior leadership needs to know how well it is communicating the values of the organization, measured by how well employees understand and believe that those values are operative. It also needs to know to what extent the organization's policies, practices, and reward systems support the appropriate values and behavior in the organization. Leadership needs effective ways of obtaining information about the various elements of the culture discussed above. Also part of the feedback mechanism is making avenues of recourse available to employees when the system breaks down and they experience unfair treatment. Most important of all, these feedback mechanisms need to become embedded in the culture itself, so that obtaining and acting on feedback becomes the normal mode of operation.

Too "Psychological"?

The topic of this book is behavioral in nature, and much of the discussion about the phenomenon itself has necessarily been focused on behavior. The suggested approach described in this chapter is also very behavior oriented. Some senior management teams may balk at the idea of working directly on some of the "soft" issues discussed here. "Our officers are not very psychologically oriented," one company officer said during a discussion of how to measure behavior that supported that company's quality initiative. This comment was made in the context of the officers getting feedback and guidance on changing their behavior. The implication was that they were willing to use an instrument with which others would evaluate their behavior, but that they were not willing to discuss how they might change. Several points must be made to counter possible objections about this approach being "too psychological."

First, if the officers are not "psychologically oriented," the question must be asked, Why not? In addition to scoping out and setting a strategic direction for an organization, what do leaders need to do? They must influence others' behavior and create conditions that maximize individual and organizational performance. All those skills involve changing behavior and stimulating learning. Behavior and learning are psychology. If one does not understand how to influence another's behavior effectively, one cannot even be a manager, much less a leader. In order to create conditions that maximize performance and influence others' behavior, one must understand the basic laws of human behavior, reviewed in Chapter 4.

Leaders must necessarily use psychology to coordinate individuals' behavior to fulfill organizational goals. No matter how leaders define their jobs, they come right down to behavior—influencing how people behave and what they do at work. Good leadership is demonstrated by someone who can take mediocre performers and turn them into star performers by creating conditions that enable them to excel, both individually and as part of an organization. Too many managers believe that their leadership skills are demonstrated when they take star performers and ferret out their weaknesses. This usually serves to turn stars into mediocre performers.

Leaders may prefer to spend their time on the strategy of guiding an organization's course. They may not want to spend significant amounts of time working on the soft issues of behavior, values, and the levels of meaning communicated through behavior. These issues may seem too subjective, too messy, to people trained to think as objectively as possible. They may expect people in the organization to deal only with objective reality. This desire is based on a rational model of how things should work; unfortunately, this is not how human beings operate. People operate on different levels of meaning. The same behavior may mean different things to different people. People infer intentions from behavior; they don't just act on the basis of the objective behavior. Chapter 1 discusses the difference between intention and impact, and how people judge the intentions of others by the impact of their behavior on them. Leaders have to understand these different levels of meaning in behavior if they want to influence people, one of the main tasks of leadership. The most effective leaders are the ones who understand and can navigate through the irrationality of human behavior.

CURRENT ORGANIZATIONAL INITIATIVES

Any discussion of organization development and cultural change would be deficient that does not mention some of the important organizational initiatives that have moved up near the top of many corporate agendas. Total quality and employee involvement, valuing and managing diversity, and work/personal life balance, to name just a few, have all become important and popular issues for organizations. All of these initiatives are relevant to the issue of employee abuse. Two aspects of these kinds of initiatives will be discussed. First, they can contribute to creating an organizational climate that supports fair treatment of employees and is incompatible with employee abuse. Second, they must be approached as part of a cultural change effort, not as a stand-alone program. Each initiative will be discussed for its applicability to the problem of employee abuse.

Total Quality and Employee Involvement

Quality is the latest catchword in American business. It is supposed to increase our productivity, make our customers love us, and position us to be globally competitive (i.e., against the Japanese). The good news is that understanding and practicing the quality framework as W. Edwards Deming (1982) originally proposed could allow us to accomplish all that and more. The bad news is that many companies have adopted certain parts of the framework—mainly the statistical tools and certain analysis techniques—in a piecemeal fashion, without adopting its underlying principles, which are the secret to quality. Deming believes that nothing short of a total transformation of management style (i.e., beliefs, values, and attitudes—in short, the corporate culture) is needed to regain American competitiveness (Deming 1982). Indeed, he has stated that American business was never truly competitive; its success after World War II was due to a sellers' market, and any system of management can succeed in a sellers' market (Walton 1986).

The principles underlying quality cause the needed changes in the corporate culture. Analysis techniques will never change the culture. Deming's entire quality approach is a systems approach. Quality is not possible without changing the underlying organizational culture. In fact, changing the culture is what quality is all about, as Deming originally conceived of it. Companies looking for easy ways to implement quality in their organizations by trying to identify the most relevant quality tools and sending everyone through training to learn to use them are making a serious mistake. The difficulty of changing the entire system (i.e., business processes and culture) is why companies that approach quality correctly find that it takes at least ten years to see progress.

Deming has also said that quality is impossible where people are afraid to tell the truth. One of his fourteen points speaks directly to that issue. He recommends that companies simply "drive out fear." He is speaking about a number of different kinds of fear: fear of job loss; fear that fixing a flawed process although improving results in the long run, will impair short-run results and therefore end in punishment; fear of helping someone else and by so doing improve that person's performance rating while worsening one's own under the individual performance rating system; and fear of not having an answer when the boss asks something. These are all fears that individuals have, but systems create and maintain these fears. The prevailing management style, the one that Deming says must be transformed, creates and maintains these fears. American management tends to rely on punishment to control and change behavior, and punishment creates fear (see Chapter 4 for a more complete discussion of how punishment is used and misused in most relationships, including work relationships).

The systems approach to quality also can contribute to an environment that does not support employee abuse. The converse of this statement is that attempts to implement quality without a comprehensive systems approach will contribute to employee abuse. Deming himself has cautioned that unless quality is approached from a systems perspective, quality could be used to intimidate and blame those lower in the organization. This obviously would create more fear and abuse. For example, another of his fourteen points is "Eliminate slogans, exhortations, and targets for the work force." Deming says that posters and exhortations are directed at the wrong people and their use arises from a misconception that quality can improve if only people worked harder. The truth is, he says, most of the trouble comes from the system itself, and so slogans like "Do it right the first time" are meaningless and completely off-target with respect to achieving quality. Slogans, exhortations, and posters generate frustration and resentment, and communicate to employees that management is unaware of the barriers they face in doing a quality job. Only management can improve the system (Deming 1982). Taking Deming's line of thinking a little further—when management's approach to quality is limited to adopting certain quality tools and training the workforce in their use, the implicit message is very similar to "Quality will improve if people just work harder," or "Do it right the first time." Management still is not taking responsibility for improving the system. It is implying that the skills of the workforce inhibit quality, not the skills of management in finding systems solutions.

Numerous references in the business press cite management's belief that poor quality is the fault of American workers. A survey of American CEOs in 1990 found that top managers in American companies believe that inadequate skills and a lack of commitment among workers are the major impediments to quality products and services. Most believe that the employees of their foreign competitors have a higher commitment to quality than do U.S. workers. As for their own role in achieving quality products and services, 62 percent believe that a lack of attention by management does not hinder quality, and 70 percent said pressure for short-term profits did not affect quality-related decisions ("Workers Get Blamed" 1990). All of these beliefs are antithetical to what Deming and other quality experts have been saying. Deming has clearly and repeatedly stated that the problem with quality is a management problem, not a workforce problem. Although it is true that the skill level of the American workforce must also be upgraded, that is not the primary factor impeding quality in this country.

As recently as 1990, Deming has said that our present system of management, by being focused on competition and judging performance, makes achieving quality impossible. American management focuses so much on competition that it continually judges its own companies' performance against the competition's, as well as judging individuals' performance against each other. This only promotes an internal focus, instead of a focus on better service to the public and to employees. Deming is very pessimistic that U.S. businesses will make the changes necessary to compete (Michaelson 1990).

Most companies are too enamored with the statistical techniques that Deming proposed to go beyond them and understand the systems perspective in which he proposed using those techniques. According to Deming, even in companies that are doing a reasonably good job of implementing quality, not much is being done to get rid of this cultural bias of internally focused competition, which will not disappear until companies cease their emphasis on rating and ranking individual performance. This focus is also responsible for much employee abuse. It directs managers toward looking for what is wrong in peoples' performance and can result in behavior that fits into several of the categories named in Chapter 1, including disrespect for and devaluation of the individual, overwork and devaluation of personal life, harassment through micromanagement, concentration on negative characteristics and failures, and management by threat and intimidation.

What approach to quality works? To determine this we must start by understanding the entire system, including those aspects of the corporate culture that contribute to creating fear in the organization. Quality and continuous process improvement depend on employee involvement and on having valid data about how things are working. Employees cannot participate and supply valid data if they fear being punished for telling the truth. By understanding the total system, top management will be better able to take the responsibility for its role in implementing quality, which is to fix the elements of the system that get in the way of workers doing their jobs.

It is important to remain open to the need to turn some elements of the system upside down—for instance, the tradition of individual performance appraisal that depends on ranking peoples' performance. Peter Block has said, "The only purpose of performance appraisals is to remind you on a yearly basis that somebody owns you" (Zemke 1991). Although this statement was made tongue-in-cheek, there is more than a grain of truth in it. Performance appraisal (evaluation of performance, merit rating, or annual review) is considered by Deming to be one of the "deadly diseases," and he says that management by fear would be a better way to describe it (Deming 1982). A system of performance appraisal creates the appropriate environment for individual abuse by providing managers with opportunities to practice management by fear. Its existence also is an example of institutional abuse, because it contributes to a culture based on management by threat and intimidation.

If one truly understands Deming's systems perspective, one cannot escape the conclusion that merit rating is unfair and based on the need to see patterns in random performance. Deming says that merit ratings reward people who do well in the system but never reward attempts to improve the system (which, incidentally, is what quality is all about). It ascribes differences to people that in reality may be caused entirely by the system in which they work. Gilovich (1991) has documented the human tendency to find patterns where only random variations exist. There is no better example of this phenomenon than in assigning performance rankings to people when circumstances beyond their control significantly affect their effectiveness. To truly create the conditions that will support an all-out effort toward continuous improvement of products and services, the annual review of individual performance will have to be given up because it drives the wrong behavior. Practicing quality appropriately will also remove opportunities for abusing employees through management by fear.

Valuing and Managing Diversity

The current approach to diversity in the workplace is evolving away from a view limited to equal employment opportunity and affirmative action considerations to a view of diversity as a strength that provides competitive advantage. The new view does not replace equal employment opportunity or affirmative action; instead it supplements and enhances its contribution. The problem with the affirmative action approach is that it is built on a model that accepts that the business mainstream, or the norm, is white male, and that therefore everyone else deviates from the norm and needs special help (Thomas 1990). The newer approach of managing diversity corresponds more closely with demographic realities and assumes that the norm is diversity, not homogeneity.

The distinction is subtle but has powerful implications. Under an affirmative action model, differences are accommodated. The expectation is that "letting in" minorities and women who might be "unqualified" could result in compromised standards, lowered performance, and less productivity. Under the managing diversity model, differences are not just accommodated but are viewed as important human resources. In this view, tapping and mining the differences among people will yield business success by increasing standards, heightening performance, and maximizing productivity.

Valuing and managing diversity means enabling every employee to perform to his or her potential. Honeywell is one example of a company that has embraced this philosophy as part of its diversity strategy. After viewing the results of an employee attitude survey, Honeywell discovered that there were no employee groups (women, minorities, members of the majority) who truly felt empowered. Senior management adopted as a goal that every employee feel empowered. In a visionary statement, Honeywell said that it aimed to create "an environment that values diversity, removes barriers to equal opportunity and empowers all employees to develop and fully utilize their unique talents, the results of which will give Honeywell a competitive advantage in the global marketplace" (Jerich 1989).

Companies that value diversity are far more likely to create an environment that supports fair treatment, enabling employees to reach their full potential, than those that simply strive to reach affirmative action goals. This kind of environment must be built if a company wants to eliminate employee abuse. Such an endeavor must be approached comprehensively in order to be integrated into the culture. Managing diversity cannot be a program that the company supports but has to be reflected in the way the company does business. A systemic approach is necessary. All aspects of the culture need to consistently emphasize the value of diversity. Values must reflect the belief, assumption, and expectation that diversity is good, desirable, and a source of strength. Everyday behavior in the organization must reflect those values. Policies, practices, systems, and rewards also must support them. Feedback from employees about how the entire system is working must be continually available so that management can effectively incorporate diversity into the culture.

To create an environment incompatible with employee abuse, one aspect of valuing diversity is perhaps the most important: enabling every employee to perform to his or her potential. What is so tragic about employee abuse is the wasted potential of those afflicted. It is not just the victim who is prevented from reaching full potential, but the abuser also. Neither individual nor organizational performance is maximized when employees are abused. Incorporating the valuing of diversity into an organization's culture will achieve maximum use of the diverse talents and abilities of employees while also creating a peak performance organizational climate incompatible with employee abuse.

Work/Personal Life Balance

Diversity in the make-up of American households has increased over the past 20 to 30 years. This has resulted in stress for increasing numbers of employees as they attempt to find a balance between work and personal life. Very few households fit the norm of the 1950s, when dad worked and mom stayed home. Today, in married households, chances are that both partners work, and that they must do so for economic reasons. Also, a larger proportion of households than in the past do not consist of a married couple with children. More single parents live with their children, and more single people live alone or with partners of the same or opposite gender.

People are living longer and marrying later, which has created another whole set of problems. The baby boom generation in particular will be faced with caring for aging parents and growing children at the same time. People coping with these demands have been termed the "sandwich generation."

These demographic and economic changes, coupled with competitive pressures that demand a greater contribution of time and energy from individuals, make it increasingly difficult to balance work and personal life. There does not seem to be enough time or resources to do both effectively. Because of the negative impact on productivity and turnover, companies have become concerned about the difficulties employees are experiencing.

How does employee abuse fit into this situation? Companies are responding to competitive pressures by demanding more time and energy from employees. Managers under pressure to produce more from their groups may show abusive behavior that could fit into any of the categories of abuse described in Chapter 1. The pressures unbalance employees' work and personal lives; the abuse they experience on top of it exacerbates the problem.

It is very fitting then that companies are taking action to ameliorate the situation for employees. If approached correctly, work/life interventions by companies could significantly help employees' lives become more balanced as well as eliminate abusive conditions in the workplace. The trick is to do it right. Again, a systems approach is necessary. The corporate culture must be examined for its contribution to the problem of work/life imbalance and related abuse. Ideally, a work/life approach is paired with an integrated quality initiative that eliminates unnecessary work and work processes. Only by addressing the conditions of overwork in the organization can the work/life imbalance problem ultimately be improved.

Without this systemic approach, interventions attempted by companies can only treat the symptoms of work/life imbalances, not the causes. It is admirable that many companies are pouring resources into increasing the supply and quality of child care in employees' communities, setting up dedicated resource and referral networks to give employees the most current information about dependent care, and even in some cases starting on-site child care centers. These resources would be necessary even if demands on employees were not excessive due to competitive pressures. However, unless the root cause of increasing time demands on employees is addressed, work/life interventions will be merely band-aid solutions. The bleeding will continue.

In order to effectively address the underlying issues, senior management needs to look at assumptions and values about employee commitment and workaholic behavior. Chapter 6 provides a good start. Leaders in all types of organizations need to open their minds to the possibility that workaholics and a workaholic culture may be worsening productivity instead of improving it. This will not be an easy task for leaders; there is a very good chance that if they have succeeded in a workaholic culture, they have strong workaholic tendencies themselves. If they can critically examine the culture in this way, and grapple with the changes in attitudes and behavior that come out of the process, the problems of employee abuse and work/life imbalance can be solved effectively—not to mention the positive by-products of improved productivity and competitiveness to be gained.

SUMMARY

The recommendations posed to senior management in this chapter will not be easy to adopt. There are no pat answers to the problems of employee abuse. This book does not provide superficial, idealistic advice like "Listen to your people more" and "Build trust." The actions that need to be taken are far more basic. The intention of this book is to provide some guidance to senior management in getting to the root causes of some very serious personnel problems.

Leaders need to start with several major tasks:

1. Understand the nature of the problem. Use data from sources named in Chapter 11 (corporate ombudsman or ethics office, employee assistance program, wellness program, union and non-union grievance systems, employee surveys). Use the classification scheme proposed in Chapter 2 to categorize the kinds of abuse prevalent in the organization. Data from the organization itself may provide other useful categories.

2. Analyze the corporate culture. Examine values, attitudes, underlying beliefs about people, and expectations about how people will behave. Examine policies, procedures, practices, and systems (e.g., development, promotion, reward, recognition, grievance, or other complaint systems) related to how employees are treated. Examine feedback and audit mechanisms that can give a reading on how well the system is working. Relate learnings about the corporate culture to the kinds of abuse discovered in Step 1.

3. Set up the appropriate mechanisms to get feedback about the organization on a continuing basis. For instance, if the organization offers no avenues of recourse for employees, establish them. If audit systems are deficient, fix them so that current data are always available.

4. Analyze current corporate initiatives (e.g., total quality). Look at the values and behavior in the organization, which surfaced in step 2, with an eye toward total quality issues. For instance, how will beliefs about people in the organization either help or hinder the development of a total quality perspective? Look at reward systems to see whether the organization is rewarding behavior consistent with a total quality approach.

5. Determine how each of these initiatives can be used to create an environment incompatible with employee abuse. Take the lead in

making necessary changes in the organization. Communicate—seek employee input and involvement. Do something unexpected, like Robert Allen did when he used electronic mail to inform and emphasize the company's policy on sexual harassment to the entire employee body of AT&T. Become a role model and ask for feedback. Use positive reinforcement to encourage those who give you feedback to continue doing so. Do not punish people who give you feedback, even if you do not like it. Clarify and communicate expectations about how managers will treat employees in the company. Make sure that organizational rewards go to people whose behavior is not abusive (remember, only their subordinates know for sure). With abusive managers, intervene but do not punish. Coach managers who need help. Make every attempt to rehabilitate, but be aware that some managers simply will not be able to fit into the new culture.

6. Keep going in the face of employee skepticism. Disbelief of your intentions is natural among employees who have been abused. It is just as natural for you to become disgusted with their seemingly negative attitude. Remember, they will need many positive experiences to cancel out the negative ones. It is important to not expect immediate results, but it is just as important to be consistent in your strategies to transform the organization.

7. Be kind to yourself when you backslide (and you will). People learning new behavior revert to old behavior when under stress. You need to try to prevent this, but you cannot always be successful. When it happens, it is of critical importance to acknowledge it and demonstrate your new awareness. If someone gives feedback about backsliding, see step 5.

There really is no alternative to working on deep cultural issues if top management wants to address the issue of employee abuse properly. The process is no more difficult and no easier than creating a quality company. The rewards in performance and profitability will be just as great.

REFERENCES

Deming, W. E. 1982. *Out of the crisis*. Cambridge, Mass.: Massachusetts Institute of Technology, Center for Advanced Engineering Study.

Gilovich, T. 1991. *How we know what isn't so: The fallibility of human reason in everyday life*. New York: Free Press.

Jerich, B. A. 1989. Address at the Conference Board's 2nd Annual West Coast Conference on Key Issues in Human Resources Management, May 10, Los Angeles.

Michaelson, G. A. 1990. The turning point of the quality revolution. *Across the Board* (December): 40–45.

Thomas, R. R., Jr. 1990. From affirmative action to affirming diversity. *Harvard Business Review* (March-April): 107–17.

Walton, M. 1986. *The Deming management method.* New York: Perigee.

Workers get blamed for impeding quality. 1990. *San Francisco Examiner* (June 27): C4.

Zemke, R. 1991. Do performance appraisals change performance? *Training* (May): 34–39.

13

A Model for Examining the Corporate Culture

In examining the culture of the organization, it is helpful to use an organizing model. This chapter provides a model that can be used to guide the leadership of an organization through an examination of its corporate culture, concentrating on the extent to which the culture supports employee abuse. This model will be especially useful to human resource managers and organization development consultants who work with client groups on organizational productivity.

Many models are available that supply a framework with which to analyze a corporate culture. This model looks at some general aspects of corporate culture that would be found in many other models. The customization of this model to the context of employee abuse is primarily in the questions that are asked about each of the various components of culture. The model also emphasizes avenues of recourse for employees to both obtain feedback about the system and provide opportunities to correct the system.

EXAMINING THE CORPORATE CULTURE

Figure 1 shows the model suggested for assessing the climate of abuse in an organization. This model includes three levels of analysis and seven components of the culture to be examined. The three levels of analysis are values, behavior, and feedback about the consistency between values and behavior. The seven components provide a comprehensive view of how values, behavior, and feedback need to be examined. The assessment begins

Figure 1
Model to Assess Organizational Climate for Abuse

Levels of Analysis	Components of the Culture	Questions to Ask
Values:	Underlying Beliefs about People	Do people tend to have intrinsic motivation, or must they be pushed? Which motivates more effectively, positive feedback about performance, or fear?
	Expectations about Peoples' Behavior	To what extent are employees out to take advantage of the system?
	Policies (How things are supposed to work)	What do we say officially about how employees should be treated? What do our policies say about handling situations of abuse and harassment? To what extent do we recognize "generic harassment" in addition to other kinds of discrimination?
Behavior:	Practices (How things really work)	To what extent do employees feel treated with dignity and respect? What happens to managers who are abusive?
	Reward Systems	What behavior is rewarded? Who gets ahead here (how do they treat subordinates?)
	Avenues of Recourse	Where can employees go for justice? What happens to employees who seek justice?
Feedback:	Audit Systems	How do we know how we're doing? How do we discover cases of abuse, their resolution, and how the employee is ultimately affected?

with a set of questions that scrutinize each of the components of the culture that contribute to its values, behavior, and feedback mechanisms.

Values

Beliefs. Everyone holds certain beliefs about people. These beliefs may be hidden, or not ordinarily available to conscious awareness. Nevertheless, they operate in our daily lives, and other people may be able to infer our beliefs about people more easily than we ourselves can. In examining this component of the culture, we need to identify what our true beliefs are about human nature, about peoples' abilities, and about our own level of trust in other people.

Some important questions to ask with regard to underlying beliefs about people are the following:

- Are talent and ability inborn or developed?
- Is it possible to type people by personality characteristics?
- Are certain personality types better, or at least better suited to the corporate environment?
- Can employee commitment to the organization be measured by the amount of time spent at work?
- Do people tend to have intrinsic motivation to do good work, or must they be pushed?
- Which is a more effective motivator, positive feedback about performance or fear?
- Are most people basically honest or dishonest?
- Are people higher in the organization more worthy individuals than people lower in the organization?
- What do I really believe about our employees' intelligence, competence, level of commitment, and character?

Expectations About Peoples' Behavior. Our beliefs about the nature of people lead us to have certain expectations about how people will behave. Those expectations in turn affect the choices we make in our own behavior. Especially if we are in a position of power over other people, it is critical that we become aware of our own expectations regarding their behavior. For instance, if I believe that people are born with certain abilities and potential, and a particular employee strikes me as not a leader type, I will not see this employee as having leadership potential. This will cause me to not expect leadership behavior from this employee. The occasions when the employee does not demonstrate leadership behavior confirm my belief. But my expectations may cause me to ignore occasions when he or she does take the lead. My faulty perception will cause me to seriously misjudge the employee and possibly fail to provide appropriate developmental experiences that could enhance his or her leadership capabilities.

Some important questions to ask with regard to expectations are the following:

- To what extent are employees out to take advantage of the system?
- To what extent is it possible to predict peoples' behavior based on certain personal characteristics?
- To what extent do we have expectations about how managers should treat employees?
- To what extent will people seek to maximize their own gain at the expense of the organization?
- To what extent am I responsible for creating an environment that makes it easy for people to behave as I want them to?
- How effectively can employees evaluate the leadership behavior of superiors?

Behavior

Policies. Every organization has some policies with regard to how people are treated. Some organizations have elaborate procedures that are written and put into some kind of management handbook. These handbooks generally contain all of the organization's administrative policies. The size of the policy binder may provide information about how employees are treated even beyond the content of the policies themselves. Highly bureaucratized organizations have rules for everything contained in fat binders. To the extent that employee treatment is bureaucratized, opportunities are provided for employee abuse, for example, a manager insisting on following procedure rather than taking responsibility for doing what is fair. Organizations with unions have another set of policies and procedures that must be followed because they are negotiated.

Beyond the daily administrative policies that determine how employees are treated is another level of policies that speak directly to abusive situations. These policies are usually handled within the framework of equal employment opportunity and deal with very specific forms of harassment and abuse; discrimination on the basis of gender, race, ethnicity, or age, and sexual harassment. Most large organizations have policies for all of these situations. Very few organizations have policies that deal with generic abuse and harassment or fair treatment in general.

Important questions to ask about policies are:

- Do we have an official policy about how we expect employees to be treated (e.g., IBM's statement about everything being done in a way to affirm the dignity of the individual)?

- What can be inferred from our administrative policies about how we expect people to be treated?

- Do we have policies with regard to the traditional forms of employee abuse (i.e., discrimination and sexual harassment)?

- To what extent do we recognize generic abuse and harassment?

- Do we have policies that deal with generic abuse?

- To what extent do we consider how employees are treated a valid business issue that must be addressed by policies?

Practices. How things really operate is often quite different from how things are supposed to operate. Policies and administrative procedures can be ignored or not followed due to lack of knowledge. They may be applied inconsistently. The pattern of policy discrepancy is very important in assessing the organizational climate and its potential for abuse. If policies are ignored, is it because managers disdain them? Because they are visionaries who cannot be bothered with bureaucratic rules? Because they do not know about them? Because the policies are complex and contradictory? If policies are applied inconsistently, is it because of favoritism, or because managers are judging each situation on its merits and sincerely trying to do the right thing?

The area of practices is the true testing ground. This is what informs employees about their value to the organization. An organization's practices will communicate to employees the extent to which they are valued and respected.

Questions that must be asked about an organization's practices include the following:

- To what extent do managers treat employees with dignity and respect?

- To what extent do employees feel treated with dignity and respect?

- To what extent do managers follow approved policies in dealing with employees?

- To what extent do managers follow established procedures, even in special situations? (i.e., to what extent are they ruled by bureaucracy rather than common sense?)

- To what extent are policies applied inconsistently?

- What are the reasons for inconsistent application?

- What happens to managers who are abusive?

- Do we even know whether or not managers are abusive?

- How much abuse is perceived by employees?

- How "level-conscious" is our culture? (E.g., are there implicit rules that govern interactions among people of different rank? For instance, is it okay to talk to people only at one's own level and one step above or below? Or can anyone in the company freely engage in discussion with anyone else, no matter what jobs they hold? Do people of different rank socialize outside of work, or do people tend to be friends only with those of the same rank? Is there a clear chain of command that is followed in formal communications?)

Reward Systems. This area of organizational behavior is very visible to employees and is often how employees judge the degree of consistency between what the organization says and what it does. The assumption employees make is that, if the organization truly values what it says it values, then the people who exemplify those values through their behavior will be rewarded (i.e., promoted). It is very difficult to fool employees, because they easily can see who gets rewarded in the organization. This is one reason why promotional decisions are so important. A promotion is not simply a way of rewarding someone who has accomplished something significant. It is a message that is sent throughout the entire organization as to what is truly valued. If the organization says that it values teamwork and consistently promotes people who are widely perceived to be team players, the message will be congruent with other messages. If, on the other hand, the organization says it values teamwork but consistently promotes people who have sabotaged others' efforts, stolen credit from others, are difficult to work with and work for, or who are glory-seekers, the message will be perceived as incongruent with other messages.

If the values communicated by promotional decisions contradict the stated values of the organization, it is clear which message will be believed by employees. Employees do not respond to a "Do as I say, not as I do" message. They look to see who gets promoted, because those decisions are perceived to be based on the real values that motivate the organization. So if the stated values are not supported by promoting people who best exemplify those values, then stating those values is a useless endeavor. At best, employees will ignore the value statements. At worst, they will scoff at them and ridicule them, and the perceived discrepancy will contribute to significant organizational dysfunction.

Questions to ask with regard to reward systems are:

• What behavior gets rewarded?
• To what extent are the behaviors that get rewarded the ones that the organization wants to reward?
• Looking at the pattern of recent promotions:

  —To what extent were these people widely perceived as demonstrating behavior consistent with what the organization says it values?
  —How do these people tend to treat subordinates?
  —What would their subordinates say about their treatment of them?

• What are the criteria upon which promotional decisions are actually made (as opposed to the criteria upon which the organization thinks they are made)? Do they include:

  —Demonstrated leadership (ability to motivate and inspire peak performance)?
  —Significant accomplishment?
  —Being in the right place at the right time?
  —Politics?

• To what extent would subordinates, superiors, and peers agree on a given manager's demonstrated leadership ability?

Feedback

Avenues of Recourse. If the system is not functioning well in supporting the dignity of the individual, employees will experience abuse. Senior leadership must be aware of this in determining the overall health of the organization. In order for senior leadership to gain access to this information, mechanisms must be in place so that employees may report instances of abuse and seek remedies. If senior leadership has no information about abusive behavior in the organization, it would be a mistake to automatically assume that it does not exist. First, an analysis must be done to determine if there are, in fact, viable reporting mechanisms. No information plus no effective mechanisms may mean that there is a significant problem with abusive behavior hidden from management's view.

Abuse is a problem that is not likely to just bubble up to the surface. Avenues of recourse must be established to deal with abusive situations and to prevent their future occurence. Some important questions to ask about avenues of recourse are the following:

• Where can employees go for justice?

• How are complaints of abuse handled?

• How effectively do the established avenues of recourse deal with abusive situations?

• What happens to employees who seek justice?

• What safeguards are built in to protect the dignity of both the abused employee and the alleged abuser?

Audit Systems. In addition to avenues of recourse, other mechanisms must be set up to get a reading on the health of the entire organization. This is especially true when the external environment is one of great change. Massive internal changes may be occurring in response to changes in the marketplace, regulation, or the competitive environment. Senior leadership needs to know how effectively they are communicating the needed changes to the employee body, as well as how employees are being affected. To what extent do policies need to be modified with regard to how people are treated? What is happening with regard to how people are really being treated? Are managers under so much pressure that they are abusing employees? How do changes in the business environment affect the behavior the organization wants to see demonstrated? To what extent is the organization successful in rewarding desired behavior? All of these questions and more need to be answered on an ongoing basis.

More specifically, how a report of abusive behavior is treated and how the employee is affected have enormous consequences with regard to the extent to which the avenues of recourse will be used. It does no good to have a mechanism for employees to report abuse if the result of reporting it is no action about the situation, and adverse consequences for the employee who reports it. After one or two instances of employees being punished for using the avenues of recourse, they will never again be used for problems of any significance.

The effectiveness of an organization's audit systems can be assessed with the following questions:

- What tools does the organization have to get feedback?

- To what extent can the organization assume that employees are telling the truth? To what extent does the system compare data from different sources?

- How does management learn about employee abuse in the organization?

- How does management learn about how cases of employee abuse are resolved?

- How does management find out how the abused employee is ultimately affected?

HOW TO USE THE MODEL

Senior leadership and human resources managers can use this model in a variety of ways. It is suggested that the senior leadership of an organization engage in analysis and discussion over a period of time. Multiple meetings and discussions will be required to integrate their own and others' viewpoints with opportunities for observation and data collection between discussions.

A facilitator is highly recommended to lead the team in using the model and focusing the discussions. The experience will be richer if the facilitator is not a member of the leadership team. Someone from outside the team can provide needed objectivity. The facilitator must find the right balance between support and confrontation. Such a task is very difficult for someone who is a part of the team. Also, if a member of the leadership team were to attempt to facilitate discussions, that person could not also participate as a member of the team. The role of facilitator is incompatible with that of participant in the process of examining the culture, and it is important for all members of the leadership team to participate together in the process.

Below is a suggested process with which to examine the organizational culture with respect to abuse. At least three meetings of the team will be needed to examine values, behavior, and feedback mechanisms, in that order. Then one or more meetings will be used to integrate learnings from the analysis of the seven components of the culture.

Recommended Process

Analyze values. Begin by answering the questions in the above sections about beliefs and expectations about behavior. Some soul-searching, and perhaps some feedback from others, will be needed to identify the real values held by members of the team. The first answer that comes to you may not be entirely accurate. Team members may need to challenge each other.

Analyze behavior. Answer the questions in the above sections about policies, practices, and reward systems in the organization. This process may demonstrate some glaring inconsistencies with values right away. If so, discuss and attempt to resolve discrepancies.

Analyze feedback mechanisms. By answering the questions above regarding avenues of recourse and audit systems, the team can begin to understand whether the organization has appropriate mechanisms in place to monitor the culture on an ongoing basis.

Go back to values and behavior. Does anything uncovered in analysis of feedback mechanisms indicate that values and behavior need to be changed? Are the organization's values and behavior consistent? Does it have the feedback mechanisms that can inform management on an ongoing basis about the congruency between organizational values and behavior? About the existence of employee abuse in the organization?

If there are feedback mechanisms available, get some data. Start with data from the sources mentioned in Chapter 11, if they exist in the organization—corporate ombudsman or ethics office, employee assistance program, wellness program, grievance system (union and nonunion), employee survey results. Are data consistent with what has been identified with regard to values and behavior? If not, what does the feedback say about how values and behavior are perceived? How is unfair treatment or employee abuse handled?

If data are inconsistent with values and behavior, re-examine values. There's a good chance that the feedback indicates the organization's true values. What must be done in order to change those values?

Re-examine behavior. What must be done to make behavior more consistent with values? Hint: Notice if the sources of data (i.e., employees) are being discounted. If you are coming up with discounting reasons, realize that doing so may say something about your values.

Cycle through this entire process as often as necessary, while implementing appropriate actions in between assessments.

If large changes are required in the organizational culture, a process like this must be used on an ongoing basis. Big changes will not be seen right away. Transforming a culture from one that is punitive and tolerates employee abuse to one that is positive and affirms the dignity of people will take some time. In fact, the process of transformation is just that—a process, not an action. The process of repeated self-examination is part of the transformation.

14

The Road Ahead

This book has explored the highly charged topic of abuse in the workplace. A wide range of abusive behavior was described, and the effects of employee abuse were analyzed in terms of costs to the business. Abuse was related to both the corporate culture and current competitive difficulties faced by American business, and an approach was suggested for tackling the problem and transforming the culture.

The seriousness of the issue is just beginning to come to light and is likely to receive more attention in the future. Employee abuse has increased in frequency and severity because of competitive pressures, but companies that tolerate abuse cannot hope to be truly competitive. There is an urgent need to raise awareness of this paradoxical situation and make the necessary changes to avert competitive troubles of crisis proportions.

Garfield (1991) believes that a transformation of the workplace is currently underway that will result in a healthier, fairer, more empowering, more productive, and more profitable enterprise. He has also stated that there will be significant resistance to this transformation, but that the changes are inevitable. The barriers he has identified are: the reluctance to apply quality principles to how people are treated, the desire to believe that leadership is limited to a few individuals rather than a potential to be nurtured in everyone, and the reliance on hierarchy in organizations. These values and beliefs are also what support abusive behavior in organizations. He calls them myths, and reports that every corporation that has challenged the myths has found them dispensable. In other words, bringing human respect and decency into the workplace turns out to be good for business.

In order to facilitate this transformation of the workplace, several efforts need to get underway.

1. Expand the concept of a "hostile work environment." One of the goals of this book is to raise awareness of generic abuse and harassment. The concept of a hostile work environment has been defined in terms of sexual harassment. Defining the qualities of a hostile work environment in this context has been instrumental in workplace efforts to ameliorate the situation for employees suffering from sexual harassment. The same needs to be done for victims of generic employee abuse. A complete understanding of what contributes to a hostile work environment is needed to develop a vision of its opposite. Strong linkages need to be established between the goals of creating an environment that eliminates the potential for abuse and creating one that facilitates quality and continuous improvement, enabling all employees to make the best use of their potential and creating a peak performance culture.

2. Expand the understanding of corporate ethics to include the ethical treatment of people. Employees must be viewed as the critical stakeholders that they are. "Good ethics is good business" applies equally well to employees as to other stakeholders. Changes are necessary in the employer/employee relationship, and organizations need to ensure that those changes are based on sound ethical principles. As part of this transformed relationship, it is necessary to move from a culture of entitlement to a culture of commitment (Bardwick 1991). Many companies have thrown out job security and along with it their philosophy of cradle-to-grave paternalism, but it is not clear what has taken its place. What appears to have been substituted, especially in employees' eyes, is a philosophy of expediency and expendability of people. Instead, a relationship of fair exchange—a new psychological contract—is needed, in which employees give top performance in exchange for opportunities to grow, develop new skills, and become more marketable. Entitlement creates loyal employees; empowerment creates committed employees. Fair treatment and empowerment lead employees to exert discretionary effort and contribute to their organization's success.

3. Develop a "moments of truth" philosophy to underly all interactions between managers and subordinates. Companies that sincerely strive to live out the people, service, profits value system tend to excel and be recognized as superior service providers. This philosophy is very consistent with the coaching role that many companies have identified as the primary role of a manager of people. The manager's job is to remove barriers for employees and facilitate their success by supplying them with what they need to do their jobs. In other words, managers need to think of

themselves as suppliers to their people, not customers. It may require a leap of faith for management to trust that if it focuses on the people in the organization, the people will focus on service to the customer, and profits will pour in. But there are enough examples of companies that tried it and saw it work that it need not be seen as such a risky proposition. Managers need to remind themselves continually that every interaction with an employee is a chance to reinforce commitment or squelch it, with a potentially significant impact on the profitability of the company.

Companies must renew their belief that their success is tied to the success of the people in the organization, as well as the other way around. The companies that have realized and acted on this knowledge have an easier time surviving in a fiercely competitive business environment. They tend to have more fun as well.

REFERENCES

Bardwick, J. M. 1991. *Danger in the comfort zone: From boardroom to mail-room—how to break the entitlement habit that's killing American business*. New York: AMACOM.

Garfield, C. 1991. Worker rights are a tool for making money. *Los Angeles Times* (November 18): B5.

Selected Bibliography

A.P.A. Task force on the prediction of dishonesty and theft in employment settings. 1991. *Questionnaires used in the prediction of trustworthiness in pre-employment selection decisions: An A.P.A. task force report.* Washington, D.C.: A.P.A. Science Directorate.

Bardwick, J. M. 1991. *Danger in the comfort zone: From boardroom to mailroom—how to break the entitlement habit that's killing American business.* New York: AMACOM.

Bernstein, A. 1991. How to motivate workers: Don't watch 'em. *Business Week* (April 29): 56.

Block, P. 1987. *The empowered manager: Positive political skills at work.* San Francisco: Jossey-Bass.

Bureau of National Affairs (BNA). 1990. *Violence and stress: The work/family connection.* Washington, D.C.: BNA PLUS Research and Special Projects Unit of the Bureau of National Affairs, Inc.

Carlzon, J. 1987. *Moments of truth.* Cambridge, Mass.: Ballinger.

Deming, W. E. 1982. *Out of the crisis.* Cambridge, Mass.: Massachusetts Institute of Technology, Center for Advanced Engineering Study.

Fassel, D. 1990. *Working ourselves to death: The high cost of workaholism and the rewards of recovery.* San Francisco: Harper & Row.

Garfield, C. 1986. *Peak Performers: The new heroes of American business.* New York: William Morrow.

Hatcher, E. 1991. Positive safety. *Training* (July): 39–41.

Kanter, R. M. 1977. *Men and women of the corporation.* New York: Basic Books.

Kupfer, A. 1988. Is drug testing good or bad? *Fortune* (December 19): 133–39.

Lee, C. 1991. What's your style? *Training* (May): 27–33.

Lombardo, M. M. and McCall, M. W., Jr. 1984. *Coping with an intolerable boss.* Greensboro, N.C.: Center for Creative Leadership.

Machlowitz, M. 1980. *Workaholics: Living with them, working with them.* Reading, Mass.: Addison-Wesley.

Makihara, M. 1991. Death of a salaryman. *In Health* (May-June): 41–50.

Mathews, M. C. 1987. Codes of ethics: Organizational behavior and misbehavior. In *Research in corporate social performance and policy,* vol. 9, edited by W. C. Frederick and L. E. Preston, 107–30. Greenwich, Conn.: JAI Press.

Milgram, S. 1963. Behavioral study of obedience. *Journal of Abnormal and Social Psychology* 67 (4): 371–78.

———. 1974. *Obedience to authority: An experimental view.* New York: Harper & Row.

Pryor, K. 1984. *Don't shoot the dog! The new art of teaching and training.* New York: Bantam Books.

Rosenbluth, H. 1991. Tales from a nonconformist company. *Harvard Business Review* (July-August): 26–36.

Ryan, K. D. and Oestreich, D. K. 1991. *Driving fear out of the workplace.* San Francisco: Jossey-Bass.

Schaef, A. W. and Fassel, D. 1988. *The addictive organization.* San Francisco: Harper & Row.

Smith, E. T. 1988. Stress: The test Americans are failing. *Business Week* (April 18): 74–76.

Strandell, B. 1991. A question of ethics. *Executive Excellence* (January): 15.

Thomas, R. R., Jr. 1990. From affirmative action to affirming diversity. *Harvard Business Review* (March-April): 107–17.

Toffler, B. L. 1986. *Tough choices: Managers talk ethics.* New York: John Wiley & Sons.

U.S. Congress, Office of Technology Assessment. 1990. *The use of integrity tests for pre-employment screening.* Washington, D.C.: U.S. Government Printing Office.

Vodanovich, S. J. and Reyna, M. 1988. Alternatives to workplace testing. *Personnel Administrator* (May): 78–84.

Walton, C. C. 1988. *The moral manager.* New York: Harper & Row.

Walton, M. 1986. *The Deming management method.* New York: Perigee.

Weisbord, M. R. 1987. *Productive workplaces: Organizing and managing for dignity, meaning, and community.* San Francisco: Jossey-Bass.

Wilson, C. B. 1991. U.S. businesses suffer from workplace trauma. *Personnel Journal* (July): 47–50.

Zimbardo, P. G.; Banks, W. C.; Haney, C.; and Jaffe, D. 1973. The mind is a formidable jailer: A Pirandellian prison. *New York Times Magazine* (April 8): 38–60.

Index

Absenteeism, 139, 142–43
Abuse: as behavior pattern, 3, 5–7,
    51; characteristics of, 4–6, 24;
    defined, xi; generic, xii–xiii, 25;
    institutional, xii; subtlety of, xi,
    xii, 6, 38; unintentional, xiv, 7,
    93, 118; verbal, 9–10, 18, 24, 44,
    45; victim-as-hostage model, 44,
    47; victims of, 4, 43–45, 46–47,
    48
Abusive behavior: connection to
    childhood abuse, 4, 45–46;
    learned, 45, 53, 60–61
Abusive behavior in workplace:
    case studies of, 7–24; creating a
    hostile work environment, xii;
    impact of, xii–xiii; by managers,
    3–4, 138; prevalence of, xi, 193;
    situational influences, 51–53
Accident records, screening, 102–3
Accidents. See On-the-job accidents
ACLU. See American Civil
    Liberties Union
Addiction to work, 81–86
Administrative slack, 149

Advancement, 28, 30, 31, 33, 34,
    40. See also Glass ceiling;
    Promotions
Affirmative action, 29, 40
Age discrimination. See
    Discrimination
Age Discrimination in Employment
    Act (ADEA), 37
Age Wave, The, 34
American Civil Liberties Union
    (ACLU), 123–24, 126, 128
American Psychological
    Association (APA), 114–15, 119
Angry outbursts, 9, 19, 24
Anxiety, 139–40, 149
Asians, 30, 32
AT&T, 178
Attitude surveys. See Employee
    surveys
Audit mechanisms, 182, 188
Authority: figures, 51, 52, 58;
    obedience to, 51–52, 62; in
    organizations, 47–49, 53
Aversive control, 57–58, 60
Avon, 32

Awards. *See* Rewards

Baby boom generation, xiv, 175
Bardwick, Judith, 194
Barriers to change, 193
Battered women, 43–45
Behavior, in model for analyzing
    culture, 166, 167–68, 181, 182,
    184–88, 190–91. *See also* Abuse;
    Abusive behavior; Abusive
    behavior in workplace
Behavioral patterns, 3, 5–7
Beliefs, 177, 182, 183
Bell Canada, 128
Benefits, 93–97, 98, 99
Blacks, 28, 30, 32
Blame, 16, 18, 21, 147, 161, 171.
    See also Fear, Intimidation
Block, Peter, 173
Bureau of National Affairs (BNA),
    3–4, 44, 45
Bureaucracy, 96, 184

Carlzon, Jan, 146
Center for Creative Leadership, 3
Change: barriers to, 193; cultural,
    165, 170; in organizations, 166,
    191; process, 191
Child abuse, 4, 44–45
Child care, 176
Coaching, 178. *See also* Mentoring
Codes of conduct. *See* Ethics, codes
    of
Codes of ethics. *See* Ethics, codes of
Coercive power, 47
Coercive tactics, 18, 58, 62. *See
    also* Intimidation; Threats
Commitment, 83, 100, 141,
    145–48, 167, 183, 194–95;
    outside the job, 147–48
Communications, formal and
    informal, 31–32
Communications Workers of
    America (CWA), 126–27. *See*

also Unions
Compensation systems. *See* Reward
    systems
Competition, 4, 80–81, 89, 172,
    175–76
Competitiveness, 4, 100, 120, 176,
    193
Conference Board, 69, 71, 123
Conflicts, 19, 57, 71, 154
Consent decrees, 33. *See also*
    Legislation
Contingent workforce, 97–100
Continuous improvement, 146,
    149–50, 161, 173, 194
Contract employees, 97
Control, need for, 24
Control: of others' behavior, 51,
    56–63; over subordinates' lives,
    48, 60. *See also* Electronic
    monitoring; Punishment;
    Surveillance
Control strategies: aversive, 57–58,
    60; positive, 57, 60
Controlling style, of managers, 19
Corning, 29, 30
Corporate culture: change effort,
    170; ethical, 68–69, 72–74;
    examining the, 163, 181–89;
    formal versus informal, 167–68;
    supporting abuse, 65, 161,
    166–68
Court decisions, 37–38
Creativity, 145; loss of, 149–50
Credibility of abused employees,
    xiii, 6, 48
Credit reporting, 125–26
Criticism, 8, 9–10, 14, 18, 142
Cultural assessment, 166, 181–82
Culture. *See* Corporate culture
Cumulative trauma disorders, 101
Customer attitudes, related to
    employee attitudes, 72
Customers: abuse of, 72, 143; poor
    relationship with, 143;

satisfaction, 72–74; satisfying versus delighting, 145–46
CWA. *See* Communications Workers of America
Cynicism, of employees, 72, 167

Death: from overwork, 88–89, 140; from stress, 140
Defensive entrepreneurs, 147
Defensiveness, 149
Degrading remarks, 9
Deming, W. Edwards, 141, 161, 170–73
Denial, 81, 89
Dependent care, 175, 176
Depression, 139
Destructive behavior, 24, 143–44
Devaluing, 7–11; of personal life, 10–11
Disabilities, 78; costs of, 138–39
Discounting, 191
Discretionary effort, 145–47, 149, 194
Discrimination, 25; age, 27, 34–38; ethnic or racial, 27, 28–33, 40; gender, 27, 33–34, 40; subtlety of, 27
Disengagement, 141, 147–48
Disrespect, 7–11
Diversity, 29–30; at Avon, 32; conventional approaches toward, 28–29, 174; at Corning, 30; in family structure, 80, 175; at Monsanto, 29–30; valuing and managing, 40, 174–75
Dominance, 47, 59–60
Downgrading, 17, 23–24
Downsizing, xiv, 23–24, 99, 100–101, 149; impact on minorities, 32–33; impact on older employees, 36–38; and overwork, 77–78, 83, 85–86; and personality testing, 118; and productivity, 85–86

Drucker, Peter, 149
Drug abuse, 108, 109, 113. *See also* Substance abuse
Drug testing, 108–13
Dual-income families, 80, 175
Dychtwald, Ken, 34–35
Dysfunctional behavior, 43, 45; brought on by stress, 46; and workaholism, 81–83

Elder care. *See* Dependent care
Electronic mail, 129–31
Electronic monitoring, 126–28
Employee abuse. *See* Abuse; Abusive behavior; Abusive behavior in workplace
Employee advocates. *See* Ombudsman
Employee Assistance Programs (EAPs), 154–55, 159
Employee benefits. *See* Benefits
Employee involvement, 89, 141, 145, 148, 170–73. *See also* Discretionary effort; Quality
Employee satisfaction: and customer satisfaction, 72–73; and Malcolm Baldridge award, 73–74
Employee surveys, 158, 160–61
Employee theft. *See* Theft, employee
Employees. *See* Workforce
Employment contract, new. *See* Psychological contract
Empowerment, 141, 145, 146, 147, 193–94
Entitlement, 194
Equal Employment Opportunity Commission (EEOC), 20, 31
Ethics: codes of, 68, 69–70; office, 68, 153–54, 158
Ethics of employee treatment, 194; and Malcolm Baldridge Award, 73–74
Ethnic and minority groups: mentoring for, 30, 31, 32; in

workforce, 28–33, 40, 174
Evaluation system. *See*
  Performance evaluation
Expectations: of employees, 71; of
  managers, 61–62, 177, 182, 183,
  190
Expert power, 47
Extra effort. *See* Discretionary effort

Fairness, 48, 70, 72, 73–74
Family responsibilities. *See*
  Dependent care; Work/life
  balance
Fassel, Diane, 81, 82, 83, 84, 85, 89
Fear: incompatible with creativity,
  149–50; incompatible with
  quality, 149–50, 171; motivating
  by, 19; in organizations, 49, 145,
  150, 161, 171; resulting from
  managerial behavior, 9, 142–43,
  149–50; of retaliation, 27, 39, 48,
  157
Federal Express, 73–74, 127–28,
  145–46, 156
Feedback, in model for analyzing
  culture, 166, 168, 177, 181–82,
  188–89, 190
Fun in work, 79

Garfield, Charles, 145
General Dynamics, 129, 154
Glass ceiling, 28–29, 33–34, 39
Global comparisons, 86–89, 100
Government agencies. *See under
  names of specific agencies*
Graphology. *See* Handwriting
  analysis
Grievances, nonunion, 156–57,
  159–60
Guest workers, 86. *See also* Illegal
  immigrants

Handwriting analysis, 118–19
Harassment, 71, 142, 157; generic,

defined, xii; verbal, 9–10, 18, 24,
  45. *See also* Abuse
Health care. *See* Managed medical
  care
Hierarchy, organizational, 47–48,
  53, 186, 193; and overwork, 80;
  prevents abuse being seen, 43,
  48, 160. *See also* Power
Hill, Anita, 39, 47
Hispanics, 30, 32
Honesty testing, 114–15
Honeywell, 174
Hostages, 44, 46–47. *See also*
  Victimization
Hostile work environment, xii,
  38–39, 194

IBM, 23, 158
Illegal immigrants, 87
Illness: job-related, 78;
  stress-related, 86–88, 97,
  138–40, 143. *See also* Managed
  medical care; Stress
Impact versus intent of behavior,
  4–5, 7, 29, 65, 169
Impulsive behavior, 24
Influence, situational, 51
Influencing others, 17–18, 56–57,
  62–63, 169
Injuries, 78, 100–104
Innovation, 149–50
Integrity testing. *See* Honesty testing
Intent of behavior. *See* Impact
  versus intent of behavior
International comparisons, 86–89,
  100
Intimidation, 17–20, 157, 171. *See
  also* Blame; Fear
Intolerable bosses, 3
Involuntary part-time work, 97–100

Japan, 86–89, 100, 170
Job engorgement, 77
Job loss, fear of, 79, 171. *See also*

Downsizing
Job pressures, 4, 138, 140
Job satisfaction: effects of
    management style on, 3; and
    medical claims, 140
Johnson & Johnson, 68

Kanter, Rosabeth, 47, 58, 82–83
Karoshi, 88–89, 140. *See also*
    Overwork; Workaholism

Labor Department. *See* U.S.
    Department of Labor
Labor force. *See* Workforce
Laws, 28, 38
Lawsuits, 140–41; against IBM, 23;
    against Merck, 30
Leadership, role of, 165–66, 177–78
Legal remedies. *See* Laws;
    Lawsuits; Legislation
Legislation, 27, 31, 33, 37, 39, 67
Legitimate power, 47
Lombardo, Michael, 3

Machlowitz, Marilyn, 81, 82, 83, 84
Managed medical care, xiii, 93–97
Management: enlightened, 145–47;
    guidance for, 177–78, 189–90;
    poor, 24, 73; senior, 165–66,
    168–70
Management development, 107, 116
Management style: effects of on
    productivity and job satisfaction,
    3; Myers-Briggs Type Indicator
    (MBTI), 116–18; negative, 4;
    role-modeling, 165–66,
    transformation of, 170–71. *See
    also* Theory X, Theory Y
Manager-employee relationship:
    abusive, 4–7; power differences
    between, xii, 48–49; supportive,
    74, 160, 194
Managers, characteristics of
    abusive, 4–7, 46

Managing diversity, 40, 174–75
Manipulating information, 13–17
Manipulation, 45
McCall, Morgan, 3
Medical benefits, 93–97. *See also*
    Benefits
Mentoring, 30, 32
Merck, 29, 30–31
Merit rating, 173. *See also*
    Performance evaluation; Rewards
Micromanagement, 11–13; of time,
    12–13; of work, 11–12
Milgram, Stanley, 51–52
Minority groups. *See* Ethnic and
    minority groups
Mistrust, 11, 12, 118, 141–42, 145,
    167
Moments of truth, 73, 194–95
Monsanto, 29–30, 103
Motivation, inference of, 5, 169
Myers-Briggs Type Indicator
    (MBTI), 116–18

Name-calling, 9
National Association for Female
    Executives, 39
Negative control. *See* Aversive
    control
Negative reinforcement, 55–56, 58
Nine to Five, 124, 126
Nonunion grievance systems. *See*
    Grievances, nonunion
Northwestern National Life
    Insurance Company (NWNL),
    138
NYNEX, 70, 154

Obedience to authority, 51–52, 62
Occupational Safety and Health
    Administration (OSHA), 101, 102
Office of Federal Contract
    Compliance, 29
Office of Technology Assessment,
    114

Older Workers Benefit Protection
    Act (OWBPA), 37
Ombudsman, 68, 71, 153–54, 158
On-the-job: accidents, 101, 102;
    illnesses, 78, 86–88; injuries, 78,
    100–104. *See also* Illness;
    Accident records, screening
Opportunities, preventing access to,
    22
Opportunity costs, 135, 137, 144–50
Organization development, xiv, 166,
    170
Organizations: commitment to, 100,
    141, 145, 167, 183, 194; loyalty
    to, 100, 194; power in, 47– 49.
    See also Commitment; Fear;
    Hierarchy, organizational
Overcontrol, 19. *See also* Control
Overevaluation, 13–17
Overtime, 10–11, 78–79
Overwork, 10–11, 77–81, 176; and
    abuse, 89; death from, 88–89,
    140. *See also* Workaholism

Pacific Bell, 32, 127
Part-time work, 97–100
Patterns of behavior, 3, 5–7, 51
Peak performance, 89, 146, 175, 194
Pentagon, 39
Performance appraisal. *See*
    Performance evaluation
Performance awards. *See* Rewards
Performance evaluation: complaints
    about, 71; current practice,
    172–73; distortion of, 23–24; and
    ethics, 70; linked to abuse,
    xii–xiii; obligation of supervisor,
    xii; and power, xii
Performance management and
    reward. *See* Performance
    evaluation; Rewards
Performance testing, 65, 111–13
Personality testing, 116–18
Physical abuse, xi, 24. *See also*

Battered women
Position power, 47
Positive control, 57, 60
Power, xii, 7; games, 5; hierarchies
    47– 48; needs, 24; in
    organizations, 43, 47– 49; social,
    47; unequal relationship, 58
Powerless, 58
Predisposition, to abuse, 24, 45, 46;
    to the negative, 61, 167
Pressure: and abuse, 4, 138; and
    suicide, 140
Prison experiment, 52–53
Privacy, 110–11, 123–24. *See also*
    Credit reporting; Drug testing;
    Electronic mail; Electronic
    monitoring; Surveillance; Voice
    mail
Procter & Gamble, 32, 129
Productivity, 35, 73, 111, 120;
    effects of management style on,
    3; global comparisons, 86–88;
    increasing, 100, 157; lowered by
    abuse, 49, 89, 132, 146, 150; and
    speed, 100; and stress, 137; and
    workaholism, 83–89, 176. *See
    also* Competitiveness; Quality
Promotions, xiii, 31, 33, 71, 186–87
Psychological contract, 194
Psychological testing, 107, 114–19.
    See also Handwriting analysis;
    Honesty testing; Personality
    testing
Punishment, 46, 47, 149, 189;
    defined, 54–55; reasons used,
    59–61; strategies, 57–58

Quality, 84–85, 89, 141– 42, 170–73

Reciprocity, 57
Recourse, avenues of, 25, 157, 166,
    168, 177, 188–89
Reference power, 47
Reinforcement: intermittent, 56;

negative, 55–56; positive, 54;
schedules, 56
Repercussions. *See* Retaliation, fear
of
Repetitive motion injuries, 101–2
Reprisal, fear of, 149, 157. *See also*
Retaliation, fear of
Resistance to change, 193
Retaliation, fear of, 27, 39, 157. *See
also* Reprisal, fear of
Revenge, 59–60, 143–44
Reverse discrimination, 28
Reward power, 47
Reward systems, 168, 177, 182,
186–88, 190
Rewards, 54, 146, 173
Rework, 84–85
Role demands, 52–53
Role modeling, 161, 165–66
Rosenbluth Travel, 74

Sabotage, 9, 143–44
Safety, 78, 100–104
Scandinavian Airline Systems
(SAS), 73, 146
Schaef, Anne, 81
Self-confidence, xi, xii
Self-doubt, 82
Self-esteem, xi, 44, 82
Self-protection, 141
Senior management: guidance for,
177–78; as role model, 71, 161,
165–66
Sexual harassment, 25, 27, 38–39,
142; hostile work environment,
xii, 38–39, 194; quid pro quo, 38
Situational influences, 51–53
Social learning, 53–56
Social power, 47
Spying. *See* Surveillance
Stanford University, 52
Stealing credit, 20–22
Stereotyping, 116–17; of older
employees, 35; of workaholics,

84
Strandell, Barbara, 4, 70
Stress, 43, 45, 46, 78; and
absenteeism, 142–43; costs of
138–40; death from, 140; and
health, 138–40; and negative
behavior or characteristics, 4;
and turnover, 142
Substance abuse, 65, 108, 110. *See
also* Drug abuse
Supervisor-employee relationship.
See Manager-employee
relationship
Supreme Court, xiv
Surveillance, 123, 128–29
Surveys. *See* Employee surveys
Systems approach, 89, 120, 161,
166, 170–73, 176

Team-building, 107
Temporary workers, 97
Testing: drug, 108–13; handwriting,
118–19; honesty, 114–15;
performance, 111–13;
personality, 116–18;
psychological, 107, 114–19
Theft, employee, 72, 114, 120
Theory X, 61–62, 167
Theory Y, 61–62
Thomas, Clarence, xiv, 39, 46
Thomas, Roosevelt, 40, 174
Threats, 17–20, 24, 46, 57
Total quality. *See* Quality
Trust: building, 177; in employees,
145; leap of faith, 195; managers
not trusting employees, 12, 167;
as part of environment, 141, 145,
149, 158
Turnover, 142

Unions, 124, 184; CWA, 126–27;
and electronic monitoring,
126–128; grievance procedures,
156

U.S. Bureau of Labor Statistics, 102
U.S. Department of Labor, 28

Values: of culture, 10, 167, 177,
    181–82; of senior management,
    166, 183–84, 190–91
Valuing diversity, 40, 174–75
Victimization, 4, 44–47, 70
Violence, 4, 43, 45
Voice mail, 131–32

Wellness programs, 155–56, 159
Wilson, C. Brady, 4, 138
Women in the workforce, 27,
    33–34, 39–40
Work, part-time, 97–100; hours
    spent, 78–81, 85, 86–89
Work/family initiatives. *See*
    Work/life balance
Work/life balance, 34, 80–81,
    175–76
Work-related: disabilities, 78;

injuries, 78, 100–104
Workaholic culture, 80–81, 176. *See
    also* Addiction to work
Workaholic organization, 82–83;
    and productivity, 83–89
Workaholics as managers, 81–82
Workaholism, 77; destructive
    effects of, 82–89, 176
Workers' compensation, 140; costs
    of, 138–39
Workforce: contingent, 97–100;
    diversity in, 40, 174–75;
    empowerment of, 141, 145, 146,
    194; ethnic and minority groups
    in, 28–33, 40, 174; older workers
    in, 35–38; part-time workers in,
    97–100; temporary workers in,
    97; women in, 27, 33–34, 39–
    40
Workplace trauma, 4, 138

Zimbardo, Philip, 52

ABOUT THE AUTHOR

EMILY S. BASSMAN is district manager with Pacific Bell in the area of Human Resource Planning. Before joining Pacific Bell, she spent ten years with AT&T, in various human resource and market research capacities. She is co-editor of *Human Resource Forecasting and Strategy Development: Guidelines for Analyzing and Fulfilling Organizational Needs* (Quorum, 1990).